Windjammer Watching
on the Coast of Maine

To Rick
Signed Dinnie Say (or Mini Dinne,
or Dinnie III - Dinnie II being my ~~great~~
aunt, or the author of this book.
Thanks for sailing, with me on
Angelique!
Dinnie

Windjammer Watching

ON THE

Coast of Maine

A Guide to the Famous
Windjammer Fleet and Other Traditional
Sailing Vessels

Virginia L. Thorndike

With Photographs by the Author

Third Edition

DOWN EAST BOOKS
Camden, Maine

Down East Books
www.nbnbooks.com
Distributed by
National Book Network

Contents

Foreword

Here on the coast of Maine we have a unique opportunity to enjoy an unusual resource: large, historic, working sailing vessels. A hundred years ago, there were thousands of such schooners; today there are only a few, though more all the time. A surprising number of them are being built, rebuilt, or converted around the planet. We are fortunate to be the home of many historic vessels and others built in traditional styles. Because there are so many here, others come. When they're in passage across this area, their captains sometimes stop in to see friends or sail in the company they find here. A rich variety of vessels comes through our waters every year. The old-time coasters, fishing vessels, pilot boats, and yachts that work in the windjammer trade represent only a few of them. Many other vessels, with a variety of histories and missions, live here on the coast or come here regularly or occasionally. It seems that nearly every interesting vessel shows up sooner or later.

In some circles, "head boats"—those that carry paying passengers—are looked down upon, as if taking tourists around were in some way a dishonorable profession. In other circles, the nonprofit vessels are equally disparaged; they are seen to be living a beggar's life. From a strictly pragmatic point of view, I don't care what the ownership or job of a vessel is as long as she remains healthy and sailing, where I can enjoy seeing her.

Whatever their missions here, the schooners and other traditional sailing vessels provide pleasure to all who see them, and each has her own interesting story. It's great sport to watch the schooners and other large sailing vessels on our coast here in Maine. This book is itself the product of my own adventures in identification and learning about the schooner fleet; I still refer to it from time to time. It has been great fun to revise the book with the perspective of more experience and knowledge of the subject than I had when I wrote the first edition in 1993.

I have found that one of the tools of windjammer watching is the VHF radio. I don't know how many times we've heard a visiting vessel call a friend on one of the local schooners, or vice versa, and thus found out what its plans were. Monitoring Channel 16 is fun even for the weather-report chatter among skippers of the local fleet.

I hope this field guide conveys both specific information (how to identify individual vessels) and a hint of the rich history that still lives on this coast.

Who's Here

Due to space concerns, the information in this book is limited to those vessels which have some public accessibility. A large number support themselves and their operators by taking people onto the water for day sails, overnight trips, or longer excursions. A variety of schools and training programs operate sailing vessels as part of the curriculum, and some vessels are on civic goodwill missions.

This book centers on the large vessels home-ported in Penobscot Bay, which continues its tradition as the center of the Maine windjammer fleet. In 2001, fifteen large schooners and a ketch sailed from Rockland, Rockport, and Camden. Penobscot Bay is also the home of Maine's official State Sailing Vessel, the schooner *Bowdoin,* which now belongs to Maine Maritime Academy and hails from Castine. I describe each of these vessels in some detail. Also provided are brief write-ups and photographs of other vessels that sail the Maine coast full- or part-time. And occasionally one comes along that, despite the questionability of her qualifications, just has to be included. The _Norfolk Rebel_ is such a vessel. Her owner is "semi-retired" and doesn't exactly offer public access, but the boat is one of a kind, she comes to Maine regularly and draws plenty of attention, and I can't imagine not including her.

There are any number of private vessels on the bays that are every bit as interesting and beautiful as many listed here, but they are beyond the scope of this guide.

Vessel Specifications

Measurements are given for length on deck, beam, and draft unless otherwise stated. Displacement is in long tons (2,240 pounds) for the vessel with half load when both light and loaded figures were known. Some of the older vessels that are "grandfathered" haven't undergone the measurements that the Coast Guard now requires for newer vessels, and their actual displacement is not known. In all cases, the information comes from the owner or the vessel Web site; I've noticed that sometimes it varies. Those who care to know to the inch or pound had better check the documentation themselves!

Terminology

Every subset of sailing folk—Gloucester fishermen, Delaware Bay oystermen, coastermen, sailors on full ships, yachting people, and so on—has its own terminology. I have made no attempt to be particularly authentic or consistent with any style; in general, I have described each vessel in the terms that her own captain used, but this effort may not have been fully successful. I apologize to anyone I may have inadvertently offended with incorrect nomenclature.

A sketch on page 144 shows the most common names for the most obvious parts of the vessels, and the glossary on page 140 defines terms that may not be familiar to all.

This matter of gender has become awkward of late. Simply for convenience I refer to a generic sailor as "he," even though in fact more and more sailors are female nowadays. I use this convention in part so as not to confuse the sailor with the vessel, which I call "her," even though I'm told it's no longer politically correct. Personally, I think that the appellation is one of respect and admiration for both vessel and gender.

A friend of mine bought a truck and called it Agatha. I remarked that a truck seems a masculine sort of vehicle, but she replied that she hadn't known where to look on a truck to ascertain its sex. I know where to look on a schooner: in the heart.

Following the example of just about everyone involved with the vessels themselves, I shall refer to them as female. Can anything with a soul be called "it"?

Acknowledgments

This book would not have been possible without the help of the owners, sailors, and followers of each vessel described. They all were generous with time and photographs, and made the research thoroughly enjoyable at all times.

Most of all, I have to thank my husband, Phil Roberts, Jr., who said that his name didn't need to appear on the cover page as long as I acknowledged that he did all the work. In spite of my directives, he got me to the right place to photograph each schooner, he was with me on all the face-to-face interviews, and he became as crazed on the subject of schooners as I did. A fellow enthusiast makes all the difference.

Schooners in the Bay

American Eagle, Roseway, Nathaniel Bowditch, Spirit of
Massachusetts, *and* J. & E. Riggin *at the finish of the 1991 Great
Schooner Race.*

Maine's coast provides extraordinary cruising ground because
of both its geography and the sailing company. Anyone spend-
ing time on the water between Bar Harbor and Boothbay will
see schooners. It's hard to make passage through Merchants
Row or Eggemoggin Reach without seeing one, and often in
Penobscot or Blue Hill Bays five or even ten big sailing vessels
may be within sight at one time, a reminder of the bygone days
of working sail. From land, too, the schooners can be seen, at
night anchored quietly in a harbor, or in the daytime perhaps
miles off, their sails bright against the sea or horizon.

"Windjammer" was once a pejorative term, used at the turn of the twentieth century by seamen on steamships to refer to those sailing craft still working. It has more recently been taken on by the cruise operators, who prefer it to the self-explanatory "dude schooner," as the earlier passenger schooners were known. (They were also called "skinboats," "head boats," and "cattle boats" in the early days of the trade. The worst name, "love barges," came during World War II, when nearly all the passengers were single women.)

The vessels in the windjammer fleet today range in age from more than 130 years to less than a decade. The older craft have worked in various capacities all along the Atlantic coast. Some were built as coasting schooners, performing the service that trucks fulfill today, carrying raw material, produce, and supplies from one coastal community to another. Others made ocean passages carrying freight. Some fished for swordfish on the Grand Banks, or for cod and mackerel, or for oysters on Delaware Bay. A couple served as pilot boats, delivering pilots to guide ships into New England ports. A few were originally built as private yachts. The *Bowdoin* was built for scientific exploration and education; although she is not now part of the windjammer fleet, she was once, and continues to make her home in Penobscot Bay. Some of the vessels had auxiliary engines when they were built; others did not but were later fitted with engines. Some, although initially designed for sail, worked primarily under power until they were reconverted to join the cruise fleet. A few have never had power, always depending on yawl boats or other external sources when their sails don't carry them where they need to go.

By the mid-1930s, sail had all but lost its commercial viability. Schooners still sailed the coast, fishing or carrying cargo

The Eva S. Cullison *at wharf, c. 1950. Penobscot Marine Museum collection, Carroll Thayer Berry photo.*

and becoming increasingly rough and tattered, but making a living was difficult. It was dangerous, too, due to lack of maintenance, which in turn was caused by the limited financial return. Captain Frank Swift saw a business opportunity in taking passengers out for cruises along the Maine coast on old working schooners. He started slowly in 1936 with a pair of small chartered vessels. The cruises caught on, and by 1939 he had a passenger waiting list for his three schooners, one of which, the *Mattie* (now called *Grace Bailey*), still carries passengers today.

Captain Swift kept adding to his fleet, and in 1948 he had nine vessels operating out of Camden. His schooners were sold or retired one by one over the years, but other captains were joining the trade. Schooners were once cheap and readily avail-

One of the "dude schooner" crews in 1954. Penobscot Marine Museum collection, Carroll Thayer Berry photo.

able, perhaps found resting next to a pier where they happened to land after their last paying trip. By the 1960s, most were beyond repair. (Wiscasset's famous hulks, the *Luther Little* and the *Hesper,* were two that weren't rescued. Generations of travelers crossing the Route 1 bridge watched them slowly collapse into the tidal flats of the Sheepscot River. Finally, in 1998, the remains were trucked off to the Wiscasset landfill.)

The first vessel built specifically for the Maine cruise business was completed in 1962. The launching of the *Mary Day* signaled a significant change in attitude; "use her up and buy another" was replaced with recognition of the value of preservation. Since then, the *Angelique, Heritage,* and *Kathryn B.* have been built for the Maine trade. Other new vessels have been and continue to be built—many of them in Maine, even though their primary sailing ground may be elsewhere—and efforts are being made countrywide to preserve other old schooners. A number of these have been found, either still working in another capacity or retired but not completely beyond hope, and with tremendous amounts of work, they have been rebuilt.

The older schooners in the Maine windjammer fleet have all had major repairs if not full rebuilds, as has the _Bowdoin_. It was said before her rebuild that if you left the _Stephen Taber_ alone for eight hours she would just gracefully go to bottom. Indeed, on one trip in the 1970s she made a stop at Billings Marine in Stonington, Maine, so that a day might be spent caulking.

Of the six windjammers operating in 1965, five still sail every week: _Grace Bailey_ (_Mattie_) and _Mercantile,_ both originally in Captain Swift's fleet; _Stephen Taber; Victory Chimes;_ and _Mary Day._ The four older schooners have been extensively rebuilt over the years, and even the then-young _Mary Day_ has now had significant work done on her, though perhaps less has been required than would be expected of a vessel nearly forty years old. The sixth, the _Adventure,_ now lives in her home port of Gloucester, Massachusetts, as a historical exhibit, and the difficult tasks of raising the money and rebuilding to bring her back to Coast Guard standards continue.

Major changes have been made in the passenger fleet and its operation since Captain Swift's early days, when no vessel carried a radio or electric power and there were no Coast Guard inspections. Passengers provided their own bedding; men slept on one side of the vessel and women on the other. Water was carried on deck, and there were few amenities. On his first passenger trip, made in 1936 in the _Annie Kimball,_ Captain Swift made a stop in Rockland to install a head. Even thirteen years later, the only power on one of Captain Swift's schooners was the 10-horsepower outboard on a skiff.

Today safety is a primary concern of schooner owners and Coast Guard alike, and the Coast Guard inspections are rigorous. Creature comforts have been improved considerably. Vessels have hot water and showers available, unheard of in coasting days. The flavor of the cruises is very different from the old days, when skippers and their crews were commercial sailors to whom the destination was the goal and the vessel merely the tool to get the passengers there. Today the purpose of the trip is the sailing itself and the enjoyment of the coast, and the vessel is cherished.

The windjammer fleet has been called a floating museum, and so it is. There are representatives from a variety of styles and functions of working sailing craft, including two schooners that have supported themselves for more than 130 years: the *Stephen Taber* and the *Lewis R. French,* the first under sail throughout, and the second in more modern adaptations as they came along. But except in the case of the *Bowdoin,* which continues to sail north into Arctic waters from time to time, a cruise today has few of the hardships of sea life a century ago. With the days of working sail that it mimics, a windjammer cruise has in common only the ocean, the hull, and the power of the wind and weather—not insignificant things to share.

Windjammer People

Every windjammer cruise is different. Some weeks offer clear northwest breezes for days on end, whereas others seem to bring more than their share of fog or rain. Wildlife spottings change from one week to another; more seals or eagles or whales are seen one week and more ospreys or porpoises or loons the next. But the biggest variable is the people, both the passengers and the schooner's own crew.

Regardless of whether the windjammer skippers came to schooners from small boats or from the merchant marine, or just grew up in the business (or in one case grew into the job from having been a passenger herself), they all love their work. They have to, or they wouldn't survive. It's an intense job during the season, with no time off-duty. The captain is responsible for the vessel at all times when she's out of port; and in the few hours between each trip's landing and the beginning of the next trip, the vessel must be maintained and reprovisioned and all shoreside business accomplished.

Of course every captain and crew member loves the sailing. Although the windjammer business is changing, with technology and materials evolving to make the experience safer and more comfortable, the actual sailing hasn't changed a bit in the century or more that some of these schooners have been working. Every skipper takes pride in sailing his vessel to the best of her capability. Informal races are common among the

schooners, and everyone knows which is the best point of sail or weather condition for each vessel. Passengers and crew both like the competition; the captains appear nonchalant, but they see everything, and the passengers enjoy the contest. They like learning how to handle the sheets and headsails to get the last bit of speed possible from each moment's changing conditions. And they all enjoy gently rubbing a competitor's nose in his schooner's defeats. One skipper whose vessel goes to windward better than off the wind enjoys quoting veteran schoonerman Captain Jim Sharp: "Even a bale of hay can go downwind."

Sometimes the competition is a little subtler. When there's no wind on a Monday morning, the Rockland fleet sometimes hangs by the breakwater, sails limp, each skipper hoping someone else will start his motor first. Or when several schooners are anchored in the same harbor on a rainy morning or a ferociously windy one, everyone keeps an eye on everyone else; if one puts up sail to move on, others feel they should, too.

Not all the sailing is fun. There are those rainy, foggy, or breezy days, and every captain has a squall story to tell. But even these stories are told with enthusiasm once the squall itself is history. One captain reports that every skipper has put his schooner aground some time or another. "How embarrassed you get depends on what the tide happens to be when you do it. I had to do it just after high tide—you don't just kedge a schooner off." Another captain doesn't admit to ever having hit the bottom, "but if we haven't been aground, it doesn't mean we haven't been embarrassed, breaking something right in front of everyone." Still another captain quotes a new skipper some years back who said that each week offered "five and a half days of pleasure and twenty minutes of sheer terror," recognizing that docking one of these large vessels, particularly those with no engine, takes tremendous skill.

The captains all enjoy being part of the history that the windjammer fleet as a whole represents. Each vessel has her own story to tell, each distinct and interesting in its own right. But when asked which schooner they would choose if they could have any in the fleet, all the skippers chose their own. (A few admitted to a nostalgic affection for the now-retired *Adventure* but still would opt for their own.)

"The passenger trade has kept these boats working in an honest business," says one captain. "None of us are getting rich, but the schooners are making a living for their owners. No one's giving fund-raising dinners to support them, and no one's taking any handouts from the government. It's free enterprise at its best."

The Maine windjammer business has kept alive the knowledge and traditions of sailing and large wooden boat maintenance that would otherwise have gone the way of so many arts and skills of the past. The windjammer fleet, dating as it does back to the days of the old coastermen, is a continuum of tradition, now another generation further down, with today's captains having learned the trade under sailors who learned from old-timers who carried cargo in schooners. Many of the captains of traditional sailing vessels throughout the United States have at one time or another worked in the Maine windjammer fleet; it is a de facto national training ground for working sailors.

Being a windjammer captain requires knowledge and interest in many fields: sailing, boatbuilding, aesthetics, and mechanics. To make a go of it, a captain must be attentive to the financial aspects of the business. But as important as any of his skills and talents is the enjoyment of people. The passengers are part of nearly every moment of the season. For many of the passengers, says one skipper, just being aboard a seagoing vessel is as foreign as being on Apollo 7. The repeat passengers act as an interface between the schooner people and the new passengers, many of whom sit aboard the night before they sail wondering whether this trip was such a good idea. The folks returning for more offer encouragement and enjoy helping the newcomers figure out how to operate the head and negotiate the companionways.

The hardest thing at first for a lot of passengers, says one captain, is that there's no schedule. "It takes them a while to understand that we really don't have a clue where we'll be anchoring, we're not just saying we don't. You can always say where we are, what direction we're headed, how fast, but not where we'll end up or when." Another captain reports, "They tease you a lot—'You don't have any idea where you're going!'—but they love it." Of course, an eye is kept to the weather, or an ear to the NOAA broadcasts, so an overnight anchorage doesn't turn into a difficult spot to get out of in the morning. But not having a fixed itinerary, being able to go wherever looks most favorable, is one of the pleasures of the windjammer cruise. "I used to worry a lot about it, where to go," says one captain, "but there's no sense in that, so you just do what you want to do. And that usually is just fine."

Few of the cruises are planned around a particular theme, or if they are, it may be for the enjoyment of the crew as much as for the passengers. In general, the personality of the captain sets the vessel's tone. Some like to "let it happen," whereas others take a more guiding role in the activities on board, leading sea chanteys, telling stories, explaining maritime conventions or nomenclature. All welcome questions and end up talking a lot about schooners, the ocean and its wildlife, islands, Maine geology, maritime history, human nature, and the state of the universe.

The hours the ship's company spends together encourage close conversation, and true friendships develop among passengers and between the schooner's crew and her customers. (How many captains over the years have ended up marrying former passengers? At least one in the current fleet.)

Reading is very common, aloud or otherwise. "One week everybody on board is reading trash," a captain reports, "and the next, they're all reading classics, three of them *War and Peace.*" At the end of a trip, while everyone else is scurrying around helping to furl sails and sharing phone numbers and addresses with one another, there's often one person sitting in a corner frantically trying to finish a murder mystery found on board. "Take it with you," says the captain. "You can send it back." (Usually that same person will have already contributed one or two books to the collection.) A few captains read aloud in the evenings: E. B. White essays, Ruth Moore's ballads, Tugboat Annie stories, or tales by Maine's seafaring people.

Stories and songs—not necessarily about the sea, though many are—are heard on board most of the vessels at one time or another. One captain says he likes to tell down east stories.

Another says his repeat customers insist that he retell the Maine tales he was brought up with, whether he wants to or not; they may have heard the stories nineteen times themselves, but they like to see the reactions of the new passengers. Another captain makes a point of sitting back and listening to his passengers' stories. Working sea chanteys are part of life on one vessel, whereas the storytelling maritime songs of Gordon Bok and Stan Rogers are common on another.

Passengers create their own themes. Common standing jokes often appear and reappear for the length of the voyage. Sometimes everyone is playing Trivial Pursuit, and other times that would be the last game anyone would want to play. Sometimes one organizer in the group, given support, can make a unique experience for all: a passenger once instigated an elaborate murder game that continued for a whole week's trip; another schooner's race effort was once supported by a loud cheerleading section led by one enthusiastic passenger.

Sometimes whatever the captain or a crew member is doing creates a storm of interest—carving wood or tying knots, for instance. On one cruise everyone got involved in making knotted mats. "One woman never did learn how to do that mat," reports a smiling former captain. "Every morning for six days I showed her, but she never did get it." A lot of brass gets polished out on the bay, too. The entire ship's company takes pride in the vessel.

Helping with the daily chores aboard is part of the experience for most passengers, although they never are required to pitch in beyond perhaps doing the initial scraping of their dishes. There's always one passenger who takes it upon him- or herself to do the dirtiest job, and it's not always who one would expect. On one trip a burly, rough-and-tough urban policeman took on the pot scrubbing after every meal; on another, the smallest, most delicate-looking woman became the official anchor-chain rinser.

Then there are the "schooner junkies," who sail as often as they can. Mattie Mosher started sailing on the cruise schooners in 1940 and says she would rather sail than eat. In 1946 she met her husband on the *Mattie* (now *Grace Bailey*), and she has sailed on her every chance she has gotten. She was given her nickname in honor of the schooner and is known as Mattie to all her friends in Maine, where she and her husband moved after his retirement in order to be near the schooners. "Whenever anyone calls and calls me Martha, I know it's someone from New Jersey," she says. Her husband died several years ago, and she still sails several times each summer. "I'd sail across the ocean in a canoe with Captain Sharp," she says. Even though he no longer sails regularly, when Sharp takes a trip to relieve one of the other captains, she's aboard. Her affection for the schooner people is reciprocated; Captain Ray Williamson, when he rebuilt the *Mattie*, hung the old name board over Mattie Mosher's bunk, and the *Grace Bailey* flies a special "Mattie is aboard" flag when Mattie's sailing. Mrs. Mosher has sailed on several other vessels as well, but it is clear that the *Mattie* is her favorite, even with her new name, *Grace Bailey*. They know each other well after half a century.

The business has changed in the last ten years; it used to be that the schooners all took on their passengers on Sunday night, sailed on Monday morning, and came back on Saturday morning. Nowadays, people can't give a whole week to one adventure, and most trips are only four nights in duration. Some schooners offer three-day trips. One captain says he won't do the shorter trips anymore. The three-day passengers never return for more, whereas those on four-day trips want more and come back. Clearly, something magical happens to the passengers on the third day.

There are many happy customers in the windjammer business, and crew members have a good time, too. Many of them are college students or young people taking time off before college or after graduation. Some are putting in time toward their own captain's license and may themselves be skippering a Maine windjammer or another commercial sailing vessel one of these days. The fleet has recently entered the fourth generation of captains, many of whom have come up through the ranks within the fleet. The old coastermen were followed by Boyd Guild, Jim Sharp, Havilah Hawkins, and their contemporaries. These captains brought along a group that have now become senior statesmen of the field: Dave Allen, Steve Cobb, Doug and Linda Lee, John Foss, and their contemporaries. As these captains retire, their vessels are being bought and sailed by younger mariners who have themselves sailed in the fleet as paid crew members prior to purchasing their own vessels.

One of these, Captain Barry King of the *Mary Day,* expressed the feelings of many of this younger generation, who all are aware of the history preceding them. "While we begin to grow into this business," he said, "our only hope is that we in some small way fill the very large shoes left for us by the Hawkinses and Cobbs and all the other captains that have put this fleet on the map. We feel excited and challenged by the responsibility to carry on a windjamming tradition that is far bigger than just us."

Design of Schooners

Note: The diagram on page 144 illustrates many of the terms used in this chapter.

New England Fishing Vessels

Early New England fishing took place close to shore, and the vessels used were small, many of them pinkies. The *Summertime* and the reproduction *Maine* both show the pinky's distinctive stern design (see pages 122 and 133).

By the middle of the nineteenth century, fishermen were going offshore to the Grand Banks, and larger, stronger, faster vessels were built. The two significant designs remaining today are the famous Gloucester fisherman *Fredonia* model from the 1880s, on whose lines the *Spirit of Massachusetts,* the *Lettie G. Howard,* and, on a miniature scale, the *Lazy Jack* were built (pages 120, 121, and 133), and the McManus-originated spoon bow of the 1890s, which typifies the last Gloucestermen. The little schooner *Surprise* was designed by McManus himself and has the look of the larger schooners. The latter are fast, seaworthy, and elegant vessels above and below the water. Their lines are graceful, from their long, overhanging bows through their sheerlines to their transom sterns. Heavy, deep keeled, and powerful, they have been cited as the most handsome and functional of sailing vessels.

In the second quarter of the twentieth century, the trend toward engine power was established. The *American Eagle* (1930) was one of the last vessels built that depended largely on sail but carried an auxiliary engine. The *Sherman Zwicker* (1942) was one of the last hybrids built; sail was used only to steady her in the winds and seas offshore (page 132).

Pilot Schooners

Even before 1800, schooners were used to put pilots aboard incoming ships to guide them into port. These schooners often represented the latest design theories for fast and seaworthy sailing vessels. Because their job was to stand by in deep water, sometimes for days on end and in all weather, they were designed to be comfortable and safe in a seaway. The *Timberwind* was specifically designed as a pilot vessel. She looks much like a Gloucester fisherman, as do the *Roseway* and *Highlander Sea,* which served the Boston pilots for more than thirty years.

The Timberwind, *heavy and deep bodied, in her former paint scheme.*

Coasting Schooners

Until after the turn of the twentieth century, nearly all material that traveled from one part of the northeastern coast of the United States to another went by schooner. Uncounted schooners were built and launched, mostly for local trips. Although some of these vessels went to the West Indies, they were not usually intended for deepwater voyages, which remained the job of the square-rigged ships. Both deep- and shallow-draft schooners were built. Because there was a practical limit to the size of two-masted schooners, three-, four-, five-, six-, and finally even a seven-master were constructed. But two-masted, shallow-draft vessels remained the norm for short hauls on the coast of Maine and in Long Island Sound, where their smaller size and shoal

The Grace Bailey, *careened for work on her hull, 1992. The coasters'
shallow draft and straight keel made it easy to beach them if necessary,
but concerns about toxicity of scraped bottom paint make it less likely
we'll be seeing schooners on the shore anymore.*

draft gave them access to harbors that larger vessels couldn't reach. Their long, straight keels allowed them to be beached for repair or so cargo could be loaded and unloaded. They were broad vessels, many with centerboards, and in summer carried topsails on each mast. In the present fleet of windjammers, the *Lewis R. French* and the *Mercantile* from Maine, the *Grace Bailey* and the *Stephen Taber* from New York, and the three-masted *Victory Chimes* from Delaware all originated as coasters. In 1962 the *Mary Day* was the first schooner of coasting design built in Maine since the *Mercantile's* Billings family launched its *Endeavor* in Stonington in 1938.

Delaware Bay Oystermen

Because of the shallowness of Delaware Bay waters, the schooners built for oystering there were constructed in a manner similar to that of the bay coasters: shallow drafted and with a long, straight keel. Today's Maine windjammer fleet includes the *Isaac H. Evans* and the *J. & E. Riggin,* both of which were built for the oyster fishery in 1886 and 1927, respectively. They are shoal-draft centerboarders that are similar beneath the waterline to their coasting cousins. The *Riggin's* more recent design is evident in her spoon bow; the *Isaac H. Evans* represents the older style.

Yachts

Although sailing for pleasure may have struck the serious merchant sailor or fisherman as foolish, the fact remains that much pleasure has been gained from (and employment given by) the sport of yachting. Yacht design since the middle of the nineteenth century has been influenced by the desire to go faster than everyone else and by well-intentioned rules meant to even out the competition. These rules have led to extremes in racing

The McManus-designed Surprise _was originally built as a yacht._

yachts and have not always led to the betterment of their sailors. But throughout the years, many cruising yachts have been designed in the fashion of the working vessels of their own or earlier days. In general, yachts were built and finished in a more refined manner than working vessels, and of course they weren't expected to carry massive amounts of cargo. The term _yachty_ is used a little derogatorily by some to describe that refinement. But in some cases it is impossible to designate a particular boat as a yacht or a working vessel—she may have functioned in both capacities at one time or another. Of the schooners in the Maine windjammer fleet today, _Nathaniel Bowditch, Ellida,_ and _Wendameen_ all started their life as yachts.

New Construction

The second half of the twentieth century saw a renewed interest in building traditional sailing vessels, a trend that continues into the twenty-first century. Several vessels are supported by a foundation, city, or nonprofit organization and were (or are being) built to serve as training or goodwill vessels; *Lynx* and the *Robert C. Seamans* are recent examples. Others belong to profit-making organizations with educational missions. One individual is responsible for the construction of six schooners, all but one named *Appledore*, which served a number of functions and are now in the day-sailing trade under various ownerships. Several vessels have been constructed for and continue to work in the passenger cruise business; four of them are in the present Maine windjammer fleet. These have been designed in a traditional style, either local (*Mary Day, Heritage,* and *Kathryn B.*) or European (the ketch *Angelique*).

Bowdoin

Note that the main is reefed. It was blowing hard that day!

The Maine State Sailing Vessel

Donald B. MacMillan was an explorer, a seaman, and a lover of living. In his time he was known to be an authority on the Labrador and Greenland coasts, often leading even local fishermen into port through fog and rocky approaches; much of today's knowledge about that area comes from his work. He was well respected for his achievements, generosity, and commitment to learning and education and to his wife, his men, his friends, and the Arctic and its people. His life was in the North, and he shared this life with the *Bowdoin*.

Designed by William Hand to MacMillan's specifications and built at Hodgdon Brothers yard in East Boothbay in 1921, the *Bowdoin* is distinct in any fleet of schooners. She was built small—for an exploration vessel—so she could hug the shoreline to avoid heavy ice and in winter be buried in the snow for insulation. She has a compact sail rig, being both bald headed and bowspritless; in the Arctic seas she sailed, where there is always either too much wind or not enough, the rig kept her crew safely aboard. She is high in the bow, to work through ice, and she carries a barrel lookout high on her foremast from which MacMillan scouted routes through pack ice.

Whereas these features can be seen from afar, some of her unique aspects aren't as apparent, and her overall ruggedness becomes obvious only on close approach. She was designed with two watertight bulkheads, so if her hull were pierced she

The Bowdoin *at Refuge Harbor, North Greenland, winter 1922–1923. Courtesy of Maine Maritime Academy.*

would remain afloat. (Such bulkheads are required now but were unusual, if not unheard of, when the *Bowdoin* was built.) Her underbody is deep and narrows as it goes down; pinched by ice, she would pop up and even fall over on her bilges if necessary, righting herself as the ice broke up. Drawing but ten feet, the average Arctic tide, she could be beached at high tide so her undersides could be worked on, and she would float herself again as the water returned. She was sheathed in an extra layer of ironwood from the waterline to four feet below as protection from the ice.

The *Bowdoin* has been well tested. On her first trip north, in 1921, she bounced off a huge solid mass of ice unscathed, and from October of that year until July 1922 she was iced in while her crew studied terrestrial magnetism and atmospheric electricity. During the winter of her second trip, she spent 330 days frozen in place at Refuge Harbor, in northern Greenland, and escaped the following summer only because she was able to break through the ice. In 1929, off Baffin Island, where the tide runs 45 feet, the *Bowdoin* and the ice mass she was anchored to were suddenly and rapidly dragged northward. MacMillan climbed up to the ice barrel lookout and saw an iceberg the size of a city block sweeping toward them, crushing smaller ice pans in its way. He commanded the crew to prepare to abandon ship. (The cook declared he was too old to die in the cold. He went below and, propping his feet against the stove, smoked a cigarette.) With the engine full ahead, Mac swung the *Bowdoin* back and forth to keep maneuvering room and at the last moment threw her hard to port. The berg scraped the starboard rail as it roared by, but the *Bowdoin* suffered no damage, and no one had to leave her.

MacMillan and the *Bowdoin* were separated during World War II. The navy sent her north while Mac worked in Washington, though both ship and captain were involved in charting Greenland. After the war, Mac found the *Bowdoin* in Boston Navy Yard—a derelict, stripped, vandalized, and filthy. Then an admiral and more than seventy years old, he worked on her himself all summer. Cummins donated an engine, and the following year the *Bowdoin* and Mac returned to the Arctic.

Mac and his schooner made twenty-six voyages north between 1921 and 1954, accompanied after Mac's marriage in the early 1930s by his wife, Miriam. At one time or another the *Bowdoin* carried scientists of a dozen different disciplines and more than three hundred students (the "*Bowdoin* boys"), who learned much about themselves, the Arctic, and life itself from her and her skipper.

When Admiral MacMillan retired, the *Bowdoin* was donated to Mystic Seaport in Connecticut, which seemed the ideal home for her, but the museum was unable to maintain her, and by 1968 she lay in a back lot under plastic, once again stripped and dying. A group of former "*Bowdoin* boys" and other enthusiasts formed the Schooner *Bowdoin* Association and brought the vessel to Camden, Maine, where Captain Jim Sharp repaired her into sailing condition. He exhibited her, carried passengers on her, and made a trip to Provincetown, Massachusetts, to allow Admiral MacMillan, then in his nineties, to once again see his vessel under sail.

A 100 percent rebuild was undertaken between 1980 and 1984, spearheaded by John Nugent and supported by many of the "*Bowdoin* boys" and other contributors. Cummins again donated an engine. Today the *Bowdoin* is as tough as ever and retains many of the features that MacMillan designed into her. She has been updated in a few areas; she carries the latest electronic gear, and her galley is far more convenient than it was in Mac's day. She still loves a good breeze; on a perfect sailing day for her, it is blowing 30 to 35 knots.

After short stints in a number of programs, including Outward Bound, in 1988 the *Bowdoin* came to Maine Maritime Academy in Castine. Captain Andy Chase, former skipper of the *Westward,* was teaching at the academy and developed a sail training program around the schooner. In 1990 Captain Chase took her back to Labrador, and in 1991 she returned to Greenland. On both trips she revisited many places she had been with Mac. The crew met people in remote villages who had known the *Bowdoin* decades before and were both amazed and thrilled to see her again. One octogenarian showed the crew a picture that MacMillan had taken of her when she was twenty-one, and a middle-aged man had a photograph of himself as an infant, given to his mother by the people on the *Bowdoin.* On these two Arctic trips, the crew was introduced to sailing conditions totally new to them. Uncharted and rocky waters, pack ice, and the complete isolation of Labrador all awed the sailors, if not the schooner.

The *Bowdoin* is now the official Maine State Sailing Vessel, having been granted this honorary title in 1986 by the state legislature and governor. Manned by many crew members who weren't even born when MacMillan last sailed her to the North, the *Bowdoin* has returned to her first workplace and is being rediscovered by old friends. Through MacMillan, the *Bowdoin* made many friends. She continues to do so as she goes on with Mac's missions of educating young people and, occasionally, Arctic adventuring.

Bowdoin
Rig: bald-headed knockabout
Sail area: 2,900 sq. ft.
White hull, spoon bow, ice barrel on foremast
Length on deck: 88'
Beam: 22'
Draft: 9'6" (full keel)
Displacement: 88 tons
Power: 190-hp Cummins diesel
No. of students: 10; crew: 5

American Eagle

The *American Eagle* is a true Gloucester fisherman. She was actually built in Gloucester (most "Gloucester" hulls were constructed in Essex, Massachusetts, and fitted out in Gloucester). The *Eagle* wasn't the most refined model of the type, and she was never intended to be a racing schooner. She was a working vessel, and she fished from Gloucester for fifty-three years, decades after the last of the racers were gone.

She was launched in 1930 as the *Andrew and Rosalie,* named for her owner's niece and nephew, whom he adopted after their father died. She was a deep-draft, oceangoing schooner carrying a four-cylinder Cooper Bessemer auxiliary engine. In 1938 the engine was upgraded to a six cylinder. Like a number of Gloucester boats during World War II, she was given a patriotic

Cape Ann, August 1977. Photo by Bill Haynes.

name to balance the fact that many of her crew were probably
not American citizens. A pilothouse was added in 1945, plunked
on top of her main cabin. Her stern was chopped off in the
fifties after a collision. When her bowsprit was no longer needed,
it was sawed off. In 1962 she was made over in the style of a
modern eastern-rig dragger: the masts were removed and a
Caterpillar engine was installed. As with many a fishing vessel
before her, her final job was as a "day boat," taken out only
when the weather looked auspicious. A day boat always was in
port at night, and maintenance was minimal.

In the late summer of 1983, after more than a half century
of fishing, she was laid up. Her present owner, Captain John

Foss, bought her about a year later. Although she was able to come to Rockland under her own power, some of her extraneous parts didn't make the whole trip. She arrived at the North End Shipyard on Halloween night. She didn't need a costume. "That old slab would make a vulture vomit," said Captain Foss's father-in-law, watching her tie up.

Boots and slickers still hung in the fo'c'sle, left from the twelve-man crews the _American Eagle_ had taken to Georges Bank in decades past. Pinholes had corroded all the way through stacks of aluminum pots and pans nested in lockers under the leaking decks. The seat lockers in the main cabin were full of gear and parts of engines long gone. The restoration project began with a great many trips to the dump.

Rebuilding took more than a year and was possible, says Captain Foss, only because he and his brother-in-law, Captain Dan Pease, were able to do the work themselves at the North End Shipyard, which Foss owned in partnership with Captains Doug and Linda Lee. Captain Foss estimates that the _American Eagle_ was 80 percent original when she was taken onto the railway. Many of her timbers and planks had to be replaced, not because of age so much as neglect; her deck hadn't been kept tight or her topsides caulked. She was still about 35 percent original on re-launch. Her stern had been returned to an approximation of its original form, and she carried a rig similar to what she had in her youth. She entered the passenger trade in 1986.

The _American Eagle_ is fun to sail, according to her skipper. She likes 12 to 20 knots of wind best, though she needn't reef before 25 knots. She's good to windward and able to point higher than many others in the fleet. Her engine, a 190-horsepower diesel, allows her to go a greater distance from home than some because there's always an easy way back. "You don't have to send the cook down in the yawl boat when the wind dies—you just turn the key." That key sends her along at 8.5 knots, but under sail she can make nearly 13 knots.

Captain Foss enjoys taking *American Eagle* back to Gloucester, which he does each Labor Day weekend for the races there. "We tie up in Gloucester, and she's not our boat anymore. She belongs to the fishermen who used to work her." Old men who sailed on her bring their whole families aboard and proudly show them around. The Piscitello brothers, who fished her from the end of World War II until she was laid up, always sail in the race itself, and usually television people come, too. The brothers take over, telling stories and keeping everyone amused. This is just fine with Captain Foss, who is free just to enjoy sailing on his schooner's home grounds.

The rewards of the windjammer business, says Captain Foss, include keeping an old vessel going and proving to the present that the past was a little more sophisticated than we sometimes think. The *American Eagle* shares her own history with her guests on every voyage.

American Eagle
Rig: bald headed, with round, tapered mastheads
Sail area: 4,600 sq. ft.
Light gray hull, blue waist, steep spoon bow
Length on deck: 92'
Beam: 20'
Draft: 11'4" (full keel)
Displacement: 107 tons
Power: 190-hp diesel
No. of passengers: 28; crew: 5

Angelique

The *Angelique* is unique among the Maine windjammers. In the first place, she is not a schooner. And she is one of only a couple with a steel hull. That's not obvious once you are aboard, however, for she has wood throughout. She was designed to resemble a Brixham trawler of the 1890s, the British counterpart of the American Gloucester fisherman. The *Angelique* is distinctive for her plumb bow, big fantail stern, dark sails, and, of course, the gaff topsail ketch rig. She would look at home in the Baltic, where the Maine schooners would look out of place.

Designed by Camden, Maine, artist Imero Gobbato and built in Florida for the Maine trade and possible cruising, the

Angelique was finished and fitted out in Maine for the 1981 season. She alone in the fleet provides an on-deck salon, which gives passengers a comfortable vantage point from which to admire the sea without being out in the weather. The cook, Deb Seip, has been aboard since the 1987 season, which was owner Captain Mike McHenry's first summer with the vessel. Deb enjoys the deckhouse, too; she says she has the best galley in the fleet and, in fact, the best workplace imaginable. Instead of being enclosed below, the cook's station is forward in the deckhouse with a beautiful view. The *Angelique's* cookstove runs on kerosene, which Deb says is easier on the cook than the woodstoves of most windjammers.

Although the *Angelique* was still very new when Captain McHenry bought her, he made a lot of renovations and changes to her that make her feel like his own vessel. He immediately repainted her in more traditional British colors. He re-sparred her, still with steel masts and wood tops, gaffs, and booms; he renovated the cabins and galley; and he put in new plumbing. He recut the topsails and headsails; she is easier to sail with just three headsails and an American-style triangular main topsail.

Perhaps the most significant change of all for the person at the helm was the removal of two big fixed propellers. These

were replaced with feathering props. "Now she sails as if someone had taken the emergency brake off," says the captain. The
informal racing among the windjammers is a good source of
pleasure for most of the skippers, who all know who's good and
what to stay away from, and when, so as not to be shown up.
"They used to come hunt me down so they could sail by me,"
Captain McHenry says, but now the *Angelique* is respected as a
fast sailer. Of course, it helps that Captain McHenry has learned
how best to sail the big ketch. He says it's not like sailing a
schooner, not only because at first it was hard for him to remember which was the mainsail and so sent his crew to adjust
the wrong canvas a few times. Because of the *Angelique's* lofty
rig, she is particularly strong to windward; when it's blowing,
her skipper loves to sheet her right in and put her on the wind.
He admits that she isn't so good downwind, when the schooners'
long booms give them a big advantage.

The *Angelique* is a strong seagoing vessel, easier to handle
offshore than a schooner with its big mainsail. She has a pair of
4-71 Detroit diesels that allow her to venture just a little farther
than she might otherwise, because if worst comes to worst, she
can always come back under power. She likes the wind best
between 12 and 15 knots, drops her jib topsail after that, but
doesn't need to strike the main and mizzen tops before 20 knots
on the wind, more than that off the wind. She's heavy enough
that she does need 5 to 6 knots to get going. On the quietest
days, when there's no wind and little prospect of much to come,
she chugs easily toward her next anchorage.

As any captain in the business must, Captain McHenry enjoys his passengers. "Windjamming is a form of camping, only
you don't have to deal with cooking and ants. The people who
come are the kind of people you'd like to have aboard." The

Angelique carries more passengers than many of the schooners in the fleet, but because of her spaciousness there always is a place to get away from everyone else. Repeat business is the base of any schooner's trade, and the *Angelique* enjoys a high rate of repeaters. The passenger list for Great Schooner Race week has some 70 percent repeaters; that trip is always the first to fill.

Although the *Angelique* has an entirely different look from the rest of the windjammer fleet, she has found respect in Maine and in the larger world of sailing, and she serves her master well.

Angelique
Rig: ketch, with three headsails and
   main and mizzen topsails
Sail area: 5,200 sq. ft.
Green hull, ivory waist, bright rail, plumb
   bow and fantail stern, tanbark sails
Length on deck: 95'
Beam: 23'7"
Draft: 11'6" (full keel)
Displacement: 140 tons
Power: two 4-71 Detroit diesels
No. of passengers: 31; crew: 5

Ellida

The most recent addition to the windjammer fleet in Penobscot Bay, *Ellida* started this phase of her career in 2000. She was
designed by John G. Alden and launched from the C. A. Morse
yard in Thomaston, Maine, in 1922, for Dr. Austen Riggs, a
pioneering psychotherapist with a treatment center in Stock-
bridge, Massachusetts. He owned the schooner only nine years
before selling her to Henry Lee Shattuck, a lawyer from Boston.
Shattuck took her to Marblehead, which she called home for
the next forty-eight years, except for a year during World War II

Ellida *at launching.*

when she was used for off-shore patrol. Shattuck had a summer home on Islesboro, and the *Ellida* spent part of each summer sailing in her present cruising ground.

In the late 1940s, *Ellida's* rig was changed. Her bow-sprit was shortened, she was given the marconi main rig she carries today, and the boomkin and backstay were added.

In 1953, she was again sold but remained in Marblehead, where Mr. and Mrs. Joseph Ballard summered on the schooner along with their cat. A fellow who ran the yacht club launch reportedly was summoned daily to take the cat ashore and bring her back again after a suitable interval.

Mr. Ballard enjoyed taking his friends for day sails, but he wouldn't wait for them. If they weren't ready to go when he was, he'd sail one circuit around the harbor; if they showed up, the launch driver would bring them to *Ellida* and somehow get them aboard as she sailed along. If the friends still hadn't appeared, Mr. Ballard would go off without them.

In 1989 the schooner again changed hands and spent ten years in Gloucester. On December 15, 1999, Captain Paul Williamson and his wife, Kris, bought her. Kris gave birth to their daughter two days later, and they found themselves with a new baby, new house, and new schooner all at once. It had been beautiful weather all month until Captain Williamson and some friends sailed her to Rockland, Maine; they endured a miserable, cold trip. She took on some water, making her new owner worry that his vessel had popped a plank, but it turned out that the problem was simply a young member of the crew failing to fully dog down a port, allowing water to come in.

The schooner is today as elegant as she was in her youth. She is set up to carry ten guests in the luxury such a yacht should offer, with gourmet meals served on china. She is elegant under way, being responsive and smooth in the water. "She's a Cadillac," says Mrs. Williamson. *Ellida's* captain adds, "With just subtle changes in the wind, she picks up speed, and she flows through the water."

She takes the seas well and enjoys a good breeze. She carries all four sails to 20 knots; over 25 knots, Captain Williamson likes to sail her under staysail and main to windward, and fore- and staysail downwind. "That's what I like about the schooner rig," he says. "You have so many different ways to split up the rig. She's handy under reefed main and staysail, but you're not limited to that." He has been changing the sail plan bit by bit; he replaced the old overlapping genoa with a smaller jib, and will add a queen top staysail—like a fisherman only triangular— to make up some of the square footage he lost, but in a more flexible format.

Ellida has an unusual windlass. You can set two batts in place and, with two people, seesaw back and forth, as is traditional, but there's an alternative on this schooner. There are pedals, and a single crew member can balance on the top and pump with his feet. "It's a 1922 Stairmaster," says Captain Williamson. Female members of the crew sometimes aren't heavy enough to operate it, though; the joke is, they have to put rocks in their pockets.

Ellida's friends from Marblehead still seek her out wherever she goes. The Williamsons' first season with her was particularly exciting when they went to Boston and Portland for the

Tall Ships festivities in those cities. *Ellida* regularly takes part in the WoodenBoat Eggemoggin Reach Regatta, as well as the various get-togethers of the schooner fleet. People recognize her all along the New England coast. There are plans for members of the Eastern Yacht Club to charter her and join the club's Maine cruise.

"You think it's your boat," says Kris, "but really they have a life of their own."

Ellida
Rig: marconi main, gaff fore
Sail area: 1,800 sq. ft.
Very dark green hull, spoon bow
Length on deck: 62'
Beam: 15'5"
Draft: 8'6" (full keel)
Power: 150-hp Perkins diesel
No. of passengers: 10; crew: 3

Grace Bailey

The *Grace Bailey*, although known for fifty years on the coast of Maine as the *Mattie,* was originally named for the builder's daughter, Grace. The vessel was built in 1882 on Long Island for sawmill owner Edwin Bailey. The finest materials were available from his yard for her construction, and even though she was supposedly rebuilt in 1906, Captain Ray Williamson, her present owner, says that when he bought her, more than a hundred years after her launching, she was 90 percent original.

The *Grace Bailey* carried hard pine from Georgia and the Carolinas to be sawn into wainscoting and other construction materials in New York City, and she made winter trips to the West Indies for fruit. When she was rebuilt or repaired in 1906, she was renamed *Mattie,* after Edwin Bailey's granddaughter,

The Mattie *fully laden. Courtesy of Captain Jim Sharp.*

Grace Bailey's niece. In 1914, the *Mattie* moved to New Haven to carry oysters on Long Island Sound.

In 1919 the *Mattie* came to Maine. When Captain H. L. Black, whose vessel had been accidentally rammed by a United States submarine, was paid by the government for his loss, he bought the *Mattie* and brought her to Bucks Harbor. Captain Black never cashed the government check, though; it was found hidden in the *Mattie's* master cabin years after he died.

The *Mattie* sailed a few trips to Massachusetts carrying boxboards, but she more often worked in Penobscot Bay carrying salt, pulpwood, coal, cod, and hardwood (as much as fifty cords at a time). She also took granite from Crotch Island to New York City to be used for the main post office and Grand Central Station. She carried a double topsail rig during this period and could move right along.

In 1938 Captain Frank Swift chartered the *Mattie* for his new passenger business. He bought her in 1940, and she has been showing passengers the best side of the Maine coast ever since, except briefly during World War II when she served as a training vessel for Maine Maritime Academy. She and the

Mercantile are the last of the schooners from Captain Swift's fleet to be still sailing.

During the vessel's last decades as the *Mattie,* she was showing her age. Her centerboard trunk leaked so much that it had been sealed up, leaving her to sail without benefit of the board. In recognition of her slowness to come around through the wind, a verse was sung about her:

Captain Fred the Mattie obeys,
But she lingers in stays for days and days.

The *Mattie* sailed under several ownerships and more captains; one, Ted Schmidt, was aboard during twenty-two years as passenger, cook, mate, and finally master. The vessel now belongs to Captain Ray and Ann Williamson's Maine Windjammer Cruises, under whose ownership she has been entirely rebuilt. And they have given her back her original name, *Grace Bailey.* The rebuilding was actually a complete restoration of the vessel. The instructions that Captain Williamson left for his project manager were simple: Put it back the way it was originally. If you take out an oak nine-by-twelve, put back an oak nine-by-twelve; if you take out a pine three-by-three, put back a pine three-by-three. This order wasn't as easy as it sounds: The *Grace Bailey* is the only member of the fleet constructed with hanging and lodging knees. You don't just walk into your local lumberyard and order a hundred knees! For each and every knee, a hackmatack tree had to be found in the woods and cut. But it was important to Captain Williamson to put the *Grace Bailey* back the way she was when first launched, and that's how she is, each gracious detail intact. Her decking is tapered, as are her cabin tops. Her main cabin paneling was taken off piece by piece; each panel was marked, then put back when the new structures were in place. Getting the old pieces to fit required a complete replication of each angle and curve of the original—no easy feat.

Like many construction jobs, this one took longer than projected. The *Grace Bailey* was re-launched on the last Friday in June of 1990. Her first cruise was scheduled for Monday. The mast was stepped on Saturday, fitting-out continued through the weekend, and on Sunday night the passengers arrived and moved into their just-finished cabins. Some thirty hired men were still caulking and rigging, and the passengers joined in and helped. The *Grace Bailey* set sail on Wednesday, July 4, and everyone enjoyed the week.

Captain Williamson wanted to share the old vessel's renewal with someone who knew her and loved her as he did. When he took a week off in the summer of 1991, he asked Captain Schmidt to return and sail as relief skipper. "Don't forget to use the centerboard!" Captain Williamson hollered out as they left. Captain Schmidt said that he enjoyed sailing the *Grace Bailey* more than he could have imagined possible. She was fast, she was light on her feet, she tracked straight. The vessel had truly been reborn.

Grace Bailey
Rig: bald headed; square mastheads
Sail area: 3,985 sq. ft.
Dark green hull, white waist, clipper bow
Length on deck: 80'   Beam: 23'6"
Draft: 7' (11'6" board down)
Displacement: 80+ tons estimated
Power: yawl boat
No. of passengers: 29; crew: 5

Heritage

The *Heritage* is the youngest wooden schooner in the Maine passenger cruise business. Her owners, Captains Doug and Linda Lee, with Captain John Foss, started North End Shipyard in Rockland in 1973. They actually reopened an old yard, installing a marine railway to replace the old one that was still there under the mud. As well as doing their own maintenance and schooner reconstructions, they rented out space for others to work on their own projects. Local vessels, both fishing and commercial boats, haul at North End now, too, and visiting schooners often are seen on the railway. By 1979 most of the major work being done to Rockland-based schooners was taking place at the North End Shipyard. Building the *Heritage* was their largest undertaking, but it was an exciting and natural next step.

The Heritage, *transom and yawl boat.*

The project was expected to take five years. The Lees sailed the *Isaac H. Evans* and Captain Foss sailed the *Lewis R. French* in summer, and they all worked on the *Heritage* during the winter. It seems that the Lees can do whatever they set their minds to; the *Heritage* is evidence of that. Captain Doug Lee designed her, chose the timber to be used for her significant structures, and, with his wife and his partner, constructed the vessel. Any iron parts that were no longer available off the shelf, including mast bands and chain plates, Captain Lee forged himself. A festive launching on April 16, 1983, was attended by a large number of enthusiasts, including representatives of all three major television networks, who happened to have been in Bath for a navy destroyer launching the day before. The Lees could more than match Bath Iron Works' claim to be on budget and on time, for the _Heritage_ was completed not only on budget but a year ahead of schedule. _Heritage_ entered the trade in June 1983.

The _Heritage_ has full headroom belowdecks and other details designed specifically for the passenger trade. Her companionway ladders are not ladders at all but stairs (no need to go down backward); she has coach houses over her galley and midships companionways (some of the charm of a historic vessel disappears when you smash your head on a companionway slide that someone has slid halfway shut). A huge skylight brightens the galley, which seats the entire ship's company at one time. Heads and the generator are housed on deck in the forward deckhouse, where any noise or fumes won't bother anyone. Two cabins have private heads, and all have hot water. Small modifications are made each year to make the vessel easier to run or more comfortable: rounding off a corner of the ice chest, improving the insulation of the chest, adding new snatch blocks to ease raising of the mainsail.

Following the old coaster tradition, the _Heritage_ carries a donkey engine, a 1917 one-lunger, which raises the anchor and can be used on the halyards on rainy days when thirty helpers aren't enthusiastic about volunteering. Like her coasting forebears, she carries a yawl boat. The challenge of sailing such a large vessel without a propelling motor is part of the appeal to her captains. She travels 150 to 200 miles a week, and although she doesn't venture beyond Schoodic Point the way the powered windjammers sometimes do, her passengers enjoy the unlimited number of little harbors and coves she visits.

A unique feature of the _Heritage,_ and indeed perhaps the very reason for her being, is the presence of the Lees' two daughters, Clara and Rachel. The Lees' first vessel, the *Isaac H. Evans*, didn't have room for the girls, who have been a part of *Heritage*'s crew every summer since they were infants. As youngsters, they operated the yawl boat, went aloft to set the topsail, and finished the sticky buns. Now, when they're not in college, Clara is deckhand/mate, and Rachel is the cook. The *Heritage* is a true family endeavor, in the tradition of many Maine coasters before her, and that is perhaps her best feature for the Lees.

Heritage
Rig: main topsail, jib topsail
Sail area: 5,200 sq. ft.
Ivory hull; white waist with red, blue,
    and black stripes; clipper bow
Length on deck: 94'
Beam: 24'
Draft: 8' (18' board down)
Displacement: 153 tons
Power: yawl boat
No. of passengers: 30; crew: 8

Isaac H. Evans

The *Boyd M. Shepard*, as the *Isaac H. Evans* was known originally, was built in Mauricetown, New Jersey, in 1886 to dredge
oysters on Delaware Bay. The life expectancy for oyster dredgers
at that time was only twenty years, but the Evans family bought
her when she was a little past that age and sailed her until 1919,
when they rebuilt her and named her for their father. She worked
until 1933, when the Depression made it no longer economical
to fish oysters, and she was beached and sunk with three other
draggers in a muddy creek. The mud protected her timbers from
destruction by freshwater woodborers. With the return of the
oyster market in 1935, she was dug out of the mud, retopped, and
put back to dragging. When oystering regulations changed in
1946, permitting full-power dredging, her masts were removed

and a pilothouse was added. Twice more she faced extensive repairs: once in 1954, after she was nearly lost during a fire at a gas
pier where she was docked, and again in 1966, when ice ripped
a plank and sank her. She went back to oystering and remained
at that job, an increasingly marginal occupation, until Doug and
Linda Lee (now the owners of the *Heritage*) bought her in 1971.

The Lees had little money at the time, but they did have
ambition, energy, and friends at the Maine Maritime Museum
in Bath, where they took the *Evans*. Over the course of a couple of years, with the help of a lot of elbow grease (that of both
the Lees and volunteers), the *Evans* was returned to her original
schooner rig. She has been sailing in the windjammer fleet since
July 1973.

The _Isaac H. Evans_ is typical of hundreds of boats built for oystering at the end of the nineteenth century and not very different from thousands of coasters, most of them long gone. In 1991 she was recognized as a National Historic Landmark representing the nineteenth-century Delaware Bay oystermen. Her age was comforting to Captain Ed Glaser, who bought her from the Lees and sailed her through 1998. "No matter what I do with her," said Captain Glaser at the time, "I'm doing something someone else has done before."

In 1995 young banker Brenda Walker had her first sail ever, an overnight trip on the _Wendameen_. She loved it so much that she left the bank, went to work on that schooner as cook, and the next year worked as mate. When a slot came open on the _Evans,_ she took that. It was a significant transition: The _Wendameen_ was her first love, and the _Evans_ was bigger, slower, and clunkier. But the old working schooner grew on her, and the longer trips felt better to her than did the _Wendameen_'s overnights. She worked for Captain Glaser for four seasons, as cook and then mate, and assumed she'd stay in that position for years to come. When Captain Glaser announced his plans to retire from the business, she found herself wondering why she couldn't buy the boat. She actually took ownership before she had her captain's license, during the winter of '99, but by sailing season she had the document and was ready to go.

"The _Evans_ is more of a matriarch," Captain Walker says. "She's a grandmother figure. She teaches me stuff all the time, from sail trim to plumbing." And, in fact, Walker has learned a great deal about the workings of large sail, both on the water and in the shipyard. She became more intimate with the innards of her schooner during the spring of 2001, when some serious work was done on the _Evans._ Although she wasn't yet ready to direct the project, she was in it all the way. Now, on a trip, she's the one who fixes the head if it clogs. That's the kind of honor that comes to the captain of a vessel, of which passengers and crew are often unaware.

But Captain Walker feels that the *Evans* takes care of her. "I've gotten myself into situations she has gotten me out of," Walker says. The schooner is very maneuverable and unusually well balanced. "It's part of the show—you can sit there and move the wheel a little and look like you're doing something, but really she's doing it all."

The *Evans* can back out of an anchorage under sail, too. Captain Walker likes to go into coves that many schooners don't attempt. And not many schooners have left Pulpit Harbor via the south side of Pulpit Rock. Unable to get out of the harbor through the regular channel in a heavy northerly blow, Captain Walker scouted the passage and marked it with buoys, leaving a channel thirty feet wide. The schooner's beam is only twenty feet—plenty of room!

"We're a good team," says Captain Walker.

Isaac H. Evans
Rig: main topsail
Sail area: 2,600 sq. ft.
White hull, black rail, clipper bow
Length on deck: 65'
Beam: 20'
Draft: 6' (14' board down)
Displacement: 68 tons
Power: yawl boat
No. of passengers: 22; crew: 4

J. & E. Riggin

The *J. & E. Riggin* is well known on Delaware Bay, and indeed has been recognized by the National Park Service as a National Historic Landmark, the best example of the twentieth-century Delaware Bay oyster dredger. She was built by Charles Riggin in Dorchester, New Jersey, in 1927 and named for his two sons, Jake and Ed. All three Riggins captained her at one time or another. She was always known as a light-air vessel, which gave her a major advantage in the short dredging season. She was also known as a fast boat; in 1929 she won the only race ever held in the bay for oystermen, thereby becoming for all time the champion bay racer!

The *Riggin* is the subject of many legends among oystermen. One, perhaps not absolutely true, tells of another vessel in the fleet headed in after the day's work, wung out and being pushed by her yawl boat, and going as fast as she possibly could. Along comes the *Riggin* from behind and goes right on by, her yawl boat still up in the davits.

In the mid-1940s, when fishing regulations changed, the oyster dredger was sold by the Riggin family and converted to power. She was taken to Long Island, where for twenty years she fished mackerel and groundfish. In 1971, still working, she was purchased by a fellow who intended to make her into an operating museum, sailing token cargo around the Cape Cod area. As in many of these projects, the expense proved to be too much and the scheme died. In 1974 the *Riggin* was again for sale, and Captain Dave Allen and his wife, Sue, made a quick trip down

The J. & E. Riggin *(foreground) with oysters piled on deck, sailing with three other oystermen in Delaware Bay around 1930. Courtesy of Captain Dave and Sue Allen.*

to Osterville, Massachusetts, hitched a ride out to look her over, chased all around town to find her owner, and agreed to buy her on the spot. They towed her bare hull back to Rockland, where they started rebuilding. It was a long process; they were doing the work themselves with the help of a number of volunteers. They did go into it with their eyes open—Captain Allen had been around other rebuilding projects that his father and other windjammer owners were involved with—but neither of them was very skilled when they started. They became more so.

Because New Jersey oystermen were intrigued that the _Riggin_ was being rebuilt, the Allens were able to obtain period equipment for her: blocks and davits, ironwork for the mast, and other gear. Dick Riggin, the son of Ed Riggin, one of the brothers for whom the _J. & E. Riggin_ was named, chased down a lot of items for the project, including the vessel's original launching pennant and forty-eight-star American flag.

The _Riggin_ was re-launched in 1977 and has been in the Maine windjammer fleet ever since. The Allens ran her for twenty years, Captain Allen in command and Sue in the galley. In 1998 she was bought by Captains Jon Finger and his wife, Anne Mahle, who continue the tradition of making their family's summer home aboard the schooner. Chloe, their elder daughter, was born soon after they bought the _Riggin,_ and Ella came along three years later.

The new captains chose the _Riggin_ specifically because she was a bald-headed centerboard boat with a yawl boat. She doesn't need topsails for speed, and the centerboard makes her handy, able to tack in a shorter distance than can a full-keel vessel. She also doesn't heel as much as a full-keel boat. Some passengers find heeling uncomfortable, and it's certainly uncomfortable for the cook when everything starts sliding off the table! Most of the captains who have yawl boats prefer them to having to maintain an engine, and risk the possibility of diesel fumes below. And the space taken up by the engine room can be better used for passengers. The yawl boat makes a convenient way to shuttle people to and from the schooner at anchor, too. Typically for a centerboard vessel with low freeboard, the *Riggin* isn't well suited to go offshore, but her captains say there's no place prettier than the coast of Maine anyway.

The *J. & E. Riggin* has a low profile, and her spoon bow is typical of the later oyster schooners on Delaware Bay. Like the coasters, she has the shallow draft and centerboard of her predecessors. Her rig has been changed since she worked in Delaware Bay; then her masts were more raked, she had a single headsail, and her main was peaked a little more. Now her sail plan looks more like that of a Maine vessel.

The *Riggin* is a fast boat, which gives her owners pleasure. In the annual Great Schooner Race, they find themselves competing against the fastest vessels, and respectably. "Some days we can pass them, some days we can't," says Captain Finger. But in the first four years they owned the *J. & E. Riggin,* she held the cup for her class three times. The *Riggin* suits her people just fine.

J. &. E. Riggin
Rig: bald headed; square mastheads
Sail area: 3,500 sq. ft.
Black hull, white rail, spoon bow
Length on deck: 89'   Beam: 22'6"
Draft: 7' (12' board down)
Displacement: 75 tons
Power: yawl boat
No. of passengers: 26; crew: 6, including a nanny

Kathryn B.

After a life in sailboats, most recently in the six-pack schooner *Memory,* Captain Gordon Baxter decided to build a bigger vessel. He and his wife (Kathryn, not surprisingly) decided that there was a niche to be filled in the Maine windjammer market for a vessel with more amenities than most of the fleet offered, more like what people expect of the charter vessels in the Caribbean. At first Baxter thought he'd build a powerboat, but after running the M/V *Pauline* for two seasons, he realized that he wasn't ready for a powerboat himself; he missed sailing. Under sail, sailing is the activity; under power, the destination and what you do when you get there are most important. More than half of his passengers on the *Pauline* said they would have preferred to be sailing, too. But they wanted a boat that carried fewer people

than most other boats in the Maine fleet, and they preferred private toilet facilities.

Thus was born the concept for *Kathryn B.*, a steel three-masted schooner designed by Tom Colvin. Captain Baxter chose steel for its strength, watertightness, ease of construction and repair, consistent quality, and price. The hull was fabricated in Florida at the Treworgy yard. Just before Christmas '95, Captain Baxter brought the powered bare hull to Maine for finishing. The trip up was no pleasure cruise, though the vessel handled it just fine. There was no rig and no interior; Captain Baxter and the two men making the delivery with him camped out in one space between the five watertight bulkheads. The weather wasn't balmy, either; fish washed on deck and froze in place, and the vessel had to break ice coming up the St. George River.

Then started the pressure of completing the interior and the rig before the season started, and the *Kathryn B.* doesn't have a simple interior. She is finished in the Victorian style with mahogany and cypress (the latter she brought north herself.) As the season came closer, Captain Baxter put out a cry for help in order to make their first charter. People came from as far away as the Caribbean to pitch in. "At one point," he says, "there were seventeen people sleeping on our living room floor." Two hours before he boarded his first passengers, the last work on *Kathryn B.* was completed. "We didn't even have a chance to raise sail to see if it fit."

Captain Baxter chose a three-masted rig for the ease of handling; *Kathryn B.* can be sailed with just two people on a watch. All the sails but the mizzen can be raised by one person; the mizzen takes two. A two-master the same size would require five people to raise the larger, heavier sails, Captain Baxter says. He wanted the schooner to be able to go anywhere; in fact, he made a round-trip to the Grenadines with her during each of her first five years in service.

She has a low, short rig that is easy to sail. "She's so well balanced you can lash the wheel and go away," says Baxter. There is no autopilot aboard, even though the schooner has made regular offshore passages. "The boat's like a tank," Captain Baxter says. She's not at her best going to windward, but offshore, "it's just a fabulous rig. She's a powerhouse off the wind." He's had her flying along at a steady 13 knots himself, and a delivery crew reported making 14 knots under double reef on her last trip back to Maine. (Baxter admits they may have gotten a push from the Gulf Stream.) She can carry her lower sails full with as much as a 30-knot wind.

But the *Kathryn B.* is best known for her amenities. She is fitted out to carry ten passengers in five bright, airy cabins, each with double bunk, private head, hand-painted pottery sink, and hot shower. One cabin can be configured as a suite for a family, bringing the passenger count to twelve. Among her crew of four are a trained chef and a stewardess. Dinner is served by candle-light. Mrs. Baxter describes the *Kathryn B.* as a "small inn afloat."

The size of the schooner makes her particularly well suited for groups who want to fill the boat with their own relations or friends. Perhaps half of her trips are filled by family groups or a number of couples who like to travel together. But even people who are strangers at the beginning of a trip know one another well by the time they're back at the dock.

Kathryn B.
Rig: three-masted schooner
Coast Guard inspected sail area: 2,700 sq. ft.
    (including five lowers and mizzen and jib
    topsails; occasionally seen with main and fore
    topsails, too, bringing her total to 3,000 sq. ft.)
Green hull, black waist, white and yellow stripes,
    clipper bow
Length on deck: 80'
Beam: 19'6"
Draft: 7'6" (fixed keel)
Displacement: 74 tons
Power: 130-hp John Deere diesel
No. of passengers: 10–12; crew: 4

Lewis R. French

Three sons of a storekeeper named Lewis R. French launched a coasting schooner in Christmas Cove, South Bristol, Maine, in 1871. They had an unwritten agreement with their father that he would help the project financially. When approached by one or another of his boys, he would say, "I'll get to it, I'll get to it," but family history says he never did. By naming the vessel the *Lewis R. French,* his sons had the last laugh, if little else; tradition says that when a vessel is named for a living person, that person supplies her with a set of flags. And Mr. French did his duty.

In the nineteenth century, as today, regulations were more demanding for vessels over 65 feet. The *French* was designed to sneak under that limit. Unlike the other coasters in the windjammer fleet, she has a fixed keel, although she draws little more than most of the centerboarders. Not having a centerboard is good for the accommodations below, which don't have to be constructed around a centerboard trunk.

The *French* has worked along the Maine coast continuously since she was launched. Of the thousands of fixed-keel coasters built in Maine during the nineteenth century, the *French* is the only one surviving. Some purists discounted her because she was converted to power; but because her owners kept up with changing times, she was able to support herself commercially for more than a hundred years. She carried general freight until

The Lewis R. French *in Northeast Harbor around 1900. Courtesy of Captain Dan Pease.*

1877, worked as a seiner out of Boothbay for four years, then returned to the coastal trade. A gasoline explosion aboard tore her up in the 1920s, when she apparently had already been modernized to the extent of having an engine along with her sails. She was rebuilt powered, with a single spar and a big wheelhouse aft. After a few years carrying lumber and coal, with Vinalhaven as home port, she was taken down east, where she worked for the sardine canneries in Eastport and Lubec. She was still carrying cannery supplies 101 years after her launching.

It is not unusual for someone to come up to the *French* at the dock, stand looking at her awhile peering this way and that, then tell how he (or his father or uncle) used to work on her. "I sure did hate loading boxes under that low deck!" said one old fellow wistfully.

Captain John Foss (now of the *American Eagle*) found the *Lewis R. French* in Eastport in 1972 and brought her to Rockland for repairs. Even though she had still been working, she was in bad shape. Some of her planking fell off as workmen reefed caulking out of the seams. Captain Foss and Doug and Linda Lee *(Heritage)* rebuilt her, returning her rig as close as they could to how it was in her youth. Captain Foss sailed her from 1976 until 1986, when Captain Dan Pease, who had crewed on her for several years, took her over. The purists can be happy today; she carries a yawl boat and has no engine aboard.

The *French* is a good sailor. Captain Pease says she goes as far as any windjammer, and her shallow draft lets him get to places that some others can't. He enjoys beating through Eggemoggin Reach with one of the deeper vessels and being able to take half as many tacks, cutting buoys and going closer to shore than they dare. He also gets a kick out of sailing under the Deer Isle bridge, which at high tide has just about as much clearance as the *French* needs. (He says that once he snapped the flag mast going under the bridge.) She likes a 15- to 20-knot breeze the best, carrying all her canvas. Her topsails allow her to do well in light airs, too. "She's pretty slippery," says Captain Pease.

The *French* has shown her ability to get through the water in recent Great Schooner Races, held annually around the Fourth of July. She has repeat passengers each year who take the race very seriously. They prepare all week, insisting on a few tacks to windward in order to practice bringing the topsail about. Since the *French's* Coaster Class starts with the captains ashore, then rowing to their vessels at the gun, a lot of work goes into boat retrieval. A bit of dinghy-racing technique paid off for the *French* in the 1991 race; even a vessel with a weight of 56 tons can be influenced by the placement of her people. Captain Pease was delighted that he was able to sneak by a competitor after the passengers all moved to leeward (a fellow passenger thought of the tactic), helping the sails to remain filled. Clearly the *Lewis R. French* and her master like to be fast.

Lewis R. French
Rig: main topsail, jib topsail
Sail area: 2,900 sq. ft.
Dark gray hull, black waist, white and
    red stripes, clipper bow
Length on deck: 64'
Beam: 19'
Draft: 7'6" (fixed keel)
Displacement: 56 tons
Power: yawl boat
No. of passengers: 23; crew: 4

Mary Day

The *Mary Day* was the first vessel built specifically for the Maine windjammer business. She reflects Captain Havilah Hawkins's lifelong love of both coasting schooners and inventive boatbuilding. It seems inevitable that, after stints in the cruise business with two other schooners, Captain Hawkins should have turned his hand to designing his own—and that she should be different from all those before her. The *Mary Day* was built in 1962 by Harvey Gamage of South Bristol, Maine. Gamage had been building large boats since World War I, but *Mary Day* was the first schooner in many years. After the *Mary Day* was launched, orders came in for several more large sailing vessels: *Shenandoah, Clearwater, Bill of Rights,* and *Harvey Gamage.* The *Mary Day* was named for Captain Hawkins's wife, a member of the well-known boatbuilding Day family from Sedgwick.

The *Mary Day*'s lines are traditional, but she is built for her present job, with a little more refinement than is found in many of the old, tough coasters and a lot more comfort. She is relatively high sided in order to provide headroom below. She has openable windows and skylights in the passenger cabins, providing light and airiness not available in the working coaster of the nineteenth and early twentieth centuries. Her main cabin is large enough to seat all the passengers at once for meals at tables grouped around a Franklin fireplace. She has companionway stairs in place of traditional ladders. Her cabin sides slant at a comfortable angle for her passengers sitting on deck to lean against.

Some of the changes to the traditional coaster that Captain Hawkins made when he designed the *Mary Day* were strictly for his and her own benefit, affecting the passengers not at all. He was tired of replacing rotted timbers in his older coasters, so he left the *Mary Day* ceilingless. He felt that constant exposure to the air would make her framing last longer—and he was right; to this day, no serious framing work has been necessary below the deckline. He wanted her cabin tops fiberglassed to prevent leakage. Her centerboard is hung in an innovative manner that makes it easier to remove and replace. And because her timbers aren't as heavy as would have been needed if she were to carry stone or be loaded to the rails with other heavy cargo, the vessel's displacement is considerably less than that of other schooners her length.

The *Mary Day* has been known as "the music boat." She carries a Blake five-stop pedal parlor organ, built in Union, Maine, probably more than a hundred years ago. Under Captain Hawkins, an important criterion in crew selection was musical ability. Gordon Bok and many other singers and instrument players worked on her; they were attracted to her and were hired because of their musicianship. Dances were held aboard; there is room on deck for a full square! And the musical tradition on the vessel continues.

The present organ is the second one on the *Mary Day;* her first burned the year the television version of *Captains Courageous* was filmed in Camden. The film crew simulated a big storm during one dramatic night scene being filmed on *Adventure,* across the harbor from the *Mary Day.* Someone admired how the *Mary Day* had been made to look as if she were on fire— only that wasn't part of the script; the *Mary Day* was indeed afire. Attributed to the spontaneous combustion of turpentine rags, the fire destroyed much of the after section below, including two cabins and the organ. Two weeks' work had her ready for the season as usual, however, though the sculpting of the fire can still be seen beneath the paint.

Captain Hawkins sailed the *Mary Day,* painted white, for twenty years, then turned her over to his son Haddie for five years, during which time she sported black paint. In 1988 Captain

Steve Cobb and his wife, Chris, bought the vessel, and she has
been painted a very light gray ever since. In 1999, after sailing her
for five years for the Cobbs, a new husband-and-wife team, Captains Barry King and Jen Martin, bought the vessel. Since then,
her bulwarks have been rebuilt, as has the transom—she is forty
years old, after all! Her present owners have made some changes
that make her their own boat, but she is still the *Mary Day.*

The *Mary Day* is the only schooner in the Penobscot Bay
windjammer fleet with a double topsail rig. She has always been
accepted as one of the faster vessels, particularly in light air. And
with the increased stability that has come with her rebuild, her
midrange has improved. She can now carry her topsails into the
15- to 20-knot range, but she is so easily driven that she doesn't
need them; she can still scoot right along without them, while
riding easier.

"I like to sail her hard," says Captain King, "but I'm not in
it for the terror, and tend to strike topsails when I see knuckles
start to whiten. It all depends on who is on board and who is in
sight. Not that I'm racing, mind you."

Mary Day
Rig: main, fore, and jib topsails
Sail area: close to 5,000 sq. ft.
Very light gray hull, cream waist, buff rail,
   clipper bow
Length on deck: 90'
Beam: 23'6"
Draft: 7' (15' board down)
Displacement: 90 tons
Power: yawl boat
No. of passengers: 28; crew: 5

Mercantile

During the winters when other employment wasn't available, the Billings family of Deer Isle built themselves schooners. Around and after World War I, they built five coastermen for various members of the family. It took more than one winter to finish the *Mercantile,* even with three generations of the family involved in the project. The lumber was sawn on-site by a wind-powered saw. They used some unorthodox construction techniques, too: some of the timbers used for her frames still had limbs on them, and as each frame was hewn out, any protruding limbs were simply cut off so the frame would butt up against the next one. The *Mercantile* was launched in 1916, and although, like most of the coasters, she had a short life expectancy, she was well (if crudely) built, for here she is today. One of the last sailing vessels built for cargo, she has sailed continuously for eighty-five years.

The *Mercantile* carried many different cargoes during nearly three decades as a Maine coasting schooner under three of the Billings brothers in succession. Her regular cargo was barrel staves and firewood for the lime kilns along the Maine coast, but each fall after the fishing season she made a number of trips from Swans Island and Frenchboro, Maine, to Gloucester, Massachusetts, carrying salt fish and bringing a little under a hundred tons of salt back for preserving the next year's catch. She carried other freight as well—lumber, coal, boxwood, and bricks—before trucks took over this job. She is said to have made one trip carrying the most dangerous cargo: unslaked lime. (More than one schooner caught fire from the intense heat of the chemical reaction caused by seawater leaking into their holds full of unslaked lime.) One night in 1939, while carrying a load of wood, the *Mercantile* collided with a steamer in the Penobscot

The Mercantile *at Old Maid's Creek in Gouldsboro, with a load of pulpwood headed for Bangor. Courtesy of the Robert Billings family.*

River and suffered considerable damage, but she was taken to Bucksport, unloaded, repaired, and put back in service.

The *Mercantile* left Maine and the Billings family early in World War II, when she was sold and taken to Rhode Island to fish mackerel. But two years later she came back to Maine when Captain Frank Swift bought her for his growing passenger trade. She has been in the cruise business ever since, under four owners and many different masters.

After three decades in the trade, the *Mercantile* was showing her age. In the 1970s a ditty was sung around the bay:

There's so much hog in the Mercantile,
They're serving pork at every meal.

Captain Les Bex raised the *Mercantile*'s stern in 1976, improving her looks and strength, and in 1989 she was fully rebuilt by her current owner, Captain Ray Williamson. By careful planning of space—rearranging cabin walls and berths and making minor adjustments to deckhouses—Captain Williamson increased the *Mercantile*'s passenger capacity by three. At the same time, he made her more comfortable, adding a third head and a shower and increasing the galley size so all the passengers can sit down to eat below. He also increased the stability of the vessel and installed holding tanks for sewage. Even from a distance, the change in the *Mercantile* after her rebuild is obvious; today her sheer is very graceful.

In the summer of 1991, the Billings family held a reunion aboard the *Mercantile*. As a young boy, Captain Bob Billings had worked on the construction of the vessel; at sixteen he had served as a deckhand. Eventually he had skippered her himself. Captain Billings and twenty-eight of his descendants came aboard for a sail, anchoring the first night in Eggemoggin Reach off the beach where she had been launched seventy-five years

The Mercantile *sailing wing and wing. This 1992 photo shows her
with her sheer restored after a major rebuilding in 1989.*

before. Billings took the wheel again during this trip, passing
under the Deer Isle bridge (which hadn't been built when they
had first sailed the reach) and into view of a huge banner: WEL-
COME HOME, CAPTAIN BOB AND THE BILLINGS
CREW!

The *Mercantile* is listed on the Register of Historic Places
and has been named a National Historic Landmark. These hon-
ors certainly recognize her national historic significance, but just
as important to the folks who care about her is her local history.
The *Mercantile* was constructed within her present cruising
ground with much local material. Into the 1980s she still carried three blocks manufactured at the Knox Mill, which stood
on the site of the Camden town pier, where she has berthed for

decades. She has spent most of her life right where she is today; she knows every little harbor from the days she carried cargo around the local bays. An old fellow from Frenchboro greeted her more than once, telling her captain how he remembered the *Mercantile* coming in for pulpwood and pointing out the wharf where she used to tie up. The *Mercantile* is a living example of coastal Maine history, and she continues to support herself and her owners as she has done now for eighty-five years.

Mercantile
Rig: bald headed; square mastheads
Sail area: 3,015 sq. ft.
Dark green hull, white waist, clipper bow
Length on deck: 80'
Beam: 22'
Draft: 6'7" (10'7" board down)
Displacement: 80+ tons estimated
Power: yawl boat
No. of passengers: 29; crew: 5

Nathaniel Bowditch

Both the *Nathaniel Bowditch* and the *Bowdoin* were designed by
William Hand and built by Hodgdon Brothers in East Boothbay, Maine, builders of many fine fishing schooners. They have
similar lines, but the *Ladonna,* as the *Bowditch* was first called, was
fitted out in 1923 as a racing yacht for Boston lawyer Homer
Loring. She was both fast and seaworthy, following the tradition
of the fishing schooners in whose form she was built, and is said
to have done well in the 1924 Bermuda Race. She was renamed
Jane Dore when she was sold to a yachtsman from the New York
Yacht Club, and in World War II she was requisitioned by the
navy to serve on submarine patrol.

After the war, the *Jane Dore* was purchased by a fisherman,
who took out her masts, installed a wheelhouse, and used her to

drag Long Island Sound for groundfish. He worked her through several years, until she was worn out, then tied her alongside some pilings in Stonington, Connecticut, where she rode up and down with the tide for a couple of years, grounding out in the muck as the water dropped and rising again as it came in.

There, in the early 1960s, her distinctive spoon bow caught the eye of schoonerman Bob Douglas. She still had the wheelhouse of a powered fishing dragger, but her bow didn't fit; it had an aristocratic look he couldn't ignore. He finally climbed aboard to see what he could see, found the documentation number on her bulkhead, wrote to Washington, and was sent her history. He tracked down the owner and bought the old vessel, rescuing her, like Black Beauty, from her desperate situation. Douglas scrounged around until he found her masts. He replaced those and started some restoration work, then sold her to Skip

On the railway, topsides scraped for her spring fitting-out, the Nathaniel Bowditch *shows off her yachty underbody.*

Hawkins, who renamed her the *Joseph W. Hawkins.* She was taken to Stonington, Maine, to be fitted for the passenger trade. But those plans didn't work out either, and she was sold again in 1971, this time to a descendant of Nathaniel Bowditch (author of the classic work on navigation) and a partner. After serious rebuilding, she was given her present name. She worked for a couple of years, but her owners "got too far ahead of their rebuild," says her present owner, Captain Gib Philbrick. Their bankruptcy left an opportunity for Captain Philbrick and his wife, Terry, who bought her in 1975 and have operated her in the windjammer business ever since.

The *Bowditch* was designed to go to weather, and go to weather she does. She likes light airs, and she likes heavy airs (there is a midrange she's not as happy with, Captain Philbrick confesses). But in a 25-knot breeze he can strike the jib and sheet the jumbo, foresail, and main right in, and she balances herself with the wind flowing smoothly from sail to sail as if she were carrying but a single sail. Then she flies to windward. In a steady breeze, some of the other windjammers can sail along with her, but in the gusty nor'westers of Penobscot Bay, her yachtlike cutaway forefoot gives her a quick handiness to take advantage of the fluky directions of the wind. None of the windjammers is likely to take on a tacking duel, but the *Bowditch* would enjoy it, being sensitive and quick to the helm. Captain Philbrick does admit that some of the coasters fare better off the wind. The *Bowditch*'s hull form makes her uncomfortable to sail wing and wing; when the straight-keeled vessels track straight, she tends to snap this way and that in the irregularities of the wind and sea. But none of the vessels is any more graceful than the *Nathaniel Bowditch,* with her elegantly curved sheer and spoon bow. She carried more canvas as a yacht, with a marconi main and staysail rig, but her sail plan today is particularly pretty, her fisherman extending the line of her jib through to the main topmast, where she carries a topsail.

The *Nathaniel Bowditch* had three careers—as yacht, submarine patrol vessel, and fisherman—then came back to find another, carrying passengers. Captain Philbrick says that you never really own one of these historic vessels, "you pass your time and try to leave them in better shape than you found them." He was reminded of his temporary part in the long life of his vessel one summer in Southwest Harbor when the granddaughter of her 1924 Bermuda Race captain rowed out and asked if she wasn't the old *Ladonna*. In another sixty years, will someone row over to her, remembering her life under Captain Philbrick?

Nathaniel Bowditch
Rig: main topsail, fisherman staysail
Sail area: 3,700 sq. ft.
Black hull, green waist, white rail, spoon bow;
    carries matching black boats on davits on
    either side
Length on deck: 82'
Beam: 21'6"
Draft: 11'
Displacement: 150 tons
Power: 4-71 Detroit diesel
No. of passengers: 24; crew: 4

Stephen Taber

"This natty little schooner promises to be a good sailer and should bring profits to her owners for years to come," said the *Long Island Gazette* when the *Stephen Taber* was launched in 1871 for the brick trade. She has most certainly done that, hauling freight around Long Island and up the Hudson River for one lifetime, being rebuilt around 1900 and working another full career carrying a variety of goods, then landing in Maine in the 1920s and continuing her labors. In 1936 Captain Fred Wood of Orland bought her and rebuilt her completely. Her graceful sheer restored, she was used for the next several years by Captain Wood and his wife to haul wood on the Penobscot River and in the bay. She often carried so many logs she nearly disappeared underneath them: sixty-three cords at a time, each weighing some two and a half tons.

Captain Boyd Guild of Castine bought her in 1946, in the early days of the Maine passenger business, but this was not the *Stephen Taber*'s first venture carrying vacationers. The summer of 1900 had been a slow time for carrying cargo on Long Island Sound, so her captain rigged the *Taber*'s forward hold with "ladies' facilities," laid out Oriental rugs and set up awnings, and took a wealthy family (complete with cook and other servants) for a month's cruise. The log shows that they fell in with a New York Yacht Club cruise to Newport and outsailed a number of the yachts, no doubt providing more pleasure to Captain Halleck and his passengers than to the yacht club members.

The Stephen Taber *entering Brooklin harbor with a load of pulpwood, 1936. Courtesy of Captain Jim Sharp.*

Unlike many of the old working schooners, the *Taber* never was converted to power. She has the distinction of being the oldest documented vessel in the United States in continuous service under sail. She is one of the smaller windjammers, 68 feet long and drawing but 5 feet with centerboard up. She was designed to get up into little coves where there was no wharf and beach out at low tide. Wagons would be run out to her, cargo would be loaded, and she would float off with the tide. She doesn't need to beach out anymore, but her shoal draft gives her access to private coves that some of the larger vessels can't reach.

Since she came into the Maine windjammer fleet, the *Stephen Taber* has introduced many a newly certified schooner captain to the emerging passenger cruise world. She served them well, or at least whetted their appetites for more, and her name appears in the resumés of many of the skippers of today's windjammers. Yet here she is today, sailing with the fleet, continuing to support herself and provide a living to her owners. Her present masters, Captains Ken and Ellen Barnes, don't see her as a stepping-stone to anywhere else, however; for historians such as themselves, she is a treasure, the quintessential coasting schooner. And she has been recognized as a National Historic Landmark.

The *Taber* has always been known as a lucky boat—lucky for her owners and lucky for herself. Whenever the time came for serious maintenance, someone loved her enough to say "Yes, she's worth it." The Barneses rebuilt her once again in the 1980s, demonstrating that rebuilding the existing schooners in the fleet was economically justified. They used old photographs and a lot of careful eyeballing to re-create the graceful sheerline that the years had taken from her. She is today as strong and capable as she ever was. She likes a good breeze; 15 to 25 knots is her forte. She reefs at 25.

She's presently painted as she was in 1871, dark green trimmed with black, red, yellow, and white—still natty. Even the angle of her gaffs is jauntily high. She's a saucy little boat with a soul that has enabled her to survive all these years. She is still a family boat, again operated by a husband-and-wife team much as she was under Captain Wood, whose widow sailed with the Barneses a number of times. In 1984, wearing a long dress, Mrs. Wood came aboard to celebrate the Bangor sesquicentennial. The Barneses had picked her up in Bucksport, where a crowd had gathered to see her off, and the _Taber_ sailed up the river. The _Mary Day_ and the _J. & E. Riggin_ also made the journey. Early the following morning, the three schooners rafted up, flying every flag they could find, yawl boats pushing, and went off with the tide, the last of uncounted gams of schooners to come down the river since the mid-nineteenth century.

The _Taber_ still carries the billet head that Orvil Young carved for her more than twenty years ago. As he was carving, an old fellow came along and admired the work, saying, "That's pretty— but she won't sail a damn bit faster."

She doesn't need to. She's fine as she is.

Stephen Taber

Rig: single topmast, no topsails
Sail area: 3,000 sq. ft.
Very dark green hull; black waist; red, yellow,
     and white stripes; clipper bow
Length on deck: 68'   Beam: 22'6"
Draft: 5' (14'6" board down)
Displacement: 73 tons estimated
Power: yawl boat
No. of passengers: 22; crew: 5

Timberwind

The *Timberwind* was built in Maine for Maine duty, and since her launching as *Portland Pilot* in 1931 she has never been out of Maine waters. Built to carry pilots to and from ships entering or leaving Portland Harbor, she was constructed ruggedly to be safe, comfortable, and seaworthy. When launched, she was bald headed, had no bowsprit, and carried two engines.

Portland Pilot and her crews faced countless vicious winter northeasters when green water as well as spray coming aboard froze to the rigging and had to be chipped off to maintain her stability. She always met the challenge, although in one particularly bitter storm, on February 16, 1958, she suffered her only casualty and was thought lost herself. The wind blew 50 knots, the seas had built to 15 feet, it was snowing, and *Portland Pilot's* dory had just left a pilot on the ladder of a fiercely rolling Norwegian ship. Each time the tanker rolled to windward, it picked up huge quantities of water; as it rolled back, the water fell in tremendous cascades over the leeward side. One such crush of water threw the pilot off the ladder. He was never seen again. The dory also was swamped and sank immediately. The two dorymen were saved by a pair of extraordinary seamen aboard the tanker, who grabbed them and hauled them aboard on the next downward roll of the ship. The weather was getting worse, visibility was zero, and the captain of the schooner, Ted Langzetell, was left alone on the *Portland Pilot*. The schooner was blown off in the storm and was not seen or heard from all night. She was feared lost. Somehow, however, she and her captain made it through the storm. The vessel was completely iced over from the seas breaking onto her, and Captain Langzetell was soaked and exhausted. He had been able to stay on deck only for short

Portland Pilot (Timberwind) *and her replacement off Portland Head, 1969. Donald E. Johnson photo.*

periods for fear of freezing, but nearly a day later the *Portland Pilot* came home under her own power.

For thirty-eight years, twenty-four hours a day, and in all weather conditions, *Portland Pilot* was on call. When she wasn't hove to on station 15 miles offshore, she was at the dock taking on stores and readying for her next shift. She was finally replaced with a steel powerboat in 1969, but to this day she is fondly remembered by the men who worked on her in Portland. They enjoy coming to Rockport to see her, and although they may chuckle at her fancier paint job and bigger rig, they see that she's still the same working vessel underneath and are pleased to know how well she's cared for.

Captain Bill and Julie Alexander bought *Portland Pilot* soon after she was retired and spent two years rebuilding her for the passenger trade. As they stripped her, they kept finding evidence of the hard life she and her crew had faced, such as elbow-length leather mittens lined with three-eighths-inch-thick wool felt. The Alexanders removed the engines and gave her a taller rig, a topsail, and a yawl boat to help out when the sails couldn't do the job. Then they fitted her out for passengers and named her *Timberwind*. They preserved as much of her original interior and fittings as they could. Even today, seventy years after her launching, a good part of *Timberwind*'s hull is still original and in near-perfect condition, having been protected by Maine's cold water.

The Alexanders sailed the *Timberwind* for twenty years, then in 1991 she came to Captain Rick Miles. Captain Miles likes the feel of the *Timberwind* under sail. She's happiest in an 18- to 20-knot breeze. Above that he strikes the topsail, and she's comfortable to 25 knots with the four lowers unreefed. The *Timberwind* is particularly handy; Captain Miles enjoys telling how her maneuverability allows him to sneak into an anchorage ahead of the larger vessels that sometimes sail by him in open water.

The *Timberwind*'s master likes the informal racing that is common in the fleet. He says the boats like it, too. He knows that a challenger might be a little faster, but there are ten different ways of getting to a destination. Local knowledge of currents, wind conditions, and even rocks and ledges may be more important than speed through the water. And the *Timberwind* can sail a little closer to the wind than some; at times that makes the difference. Says Miles, "No one's going to get by without us having done our best."

Captain Miles has sailed all his life, and to him the *Timberwind* is a dream come true. Although he loves all boats, believing in an almost mystical connection between any vessel and her captain, the *Timberwind* is special to him: her history, her physical characteristics, her sailing abilities—and her soul. The *Timberwind* has spent her life with masters who loved her and respected her, and her latest captain is as enamored of her as any.

Timberwind

Rig: single topsail

Sail area: 2,520 sq. ft.

White hull, gray rail, steep spoon bow

Length on deck: 70'

Beam: 18'6"

Draft: 9'7" (full keel)

Displacement: 85 tons

Power: yawl boat

No. of passengers: 20; crew: 4

Victory Chimes

The *Victory Chimes* was built as the *Edwin and Maud* in Bethel, Delaware, in 1900. Named for the children of Robert Riggin, her first captain (and cousin of the first owner of the *J. & E. Riggin*), she is a ram schooner, thirty-nine of which were built for the waters of Chesapeake Bay. No one agrees on the derivation of the term *ram schooner*—it may have been a derogatory phrase referring to the way these vessels passed through the water—but the schooners are said to have earned more money for their owners than any other three-masted schooners. Despite their great size, they were sailed with a crew of just three or four men, because all the sails save a headsail were self-tending. Only the *Victory Chimes* remains; in fact, she is the last original three-masted schooner working in the United States.

The *Edwin and Maud* was designed to carry the maximum load through the Chesapeake and Delaware Canal, the vessel being just inches narrower than the canal itself. She is flat bottomed and flat sided; at 170 feet long, including her bowsprit, she is probably just as long as she could be and still get through the locks. She draws only 7.5 feet of water with her centerboard up. She was built sturdy to carry huge cargoes; her skipper, Captain Kip Files, says she used to carry 60 to 70 tons on deck alone. She is massively overbuilt for her present job.

The *Edwin and Maud* worked for more than forty years carrying cargo and for several years carrying passengers on the Chesapeake before Captain Boyd Guild brought her to Maine in 1954 and gave her the name *Victory Chimes*. She cruised in Maine for thirty years.

The Victory Chimes *on the railway, showing her boxy hull shape, designed for maximum cargo capacity.*

In 1985 she was purchased and taken to the Great Lakes, where she came on hard times and was ultimately repossessed by a Duluth bank. Her next stop was home on the Chesapeake, where she was offered for sale. There she sat, her pumps running around the clock to keep her afloat. She was finally rescued when Thomas Monaghan of Domino's Pizza bought her. During the three years that Domino's owned her, a great deal of careful restoration work was done.

The *Victory Chimes*'s three masts stand some 80 feet over the water. Replacing one of these was not an easy matter, at least not in the original single-log style. A straight tree 100 feet tall was required to get a 21-inch diameter that extended the necessary length. But there was no skimping of materials during her restoration.

Much to the distress of folks who knew her as the *Victory Chimes,* the vessel carried the name *Domino Effect* during the years she belonged to Domino's. (On the Cheasapeake, people are just as upset by the name *Victory Chimes,* because she had been well known there as the *Edwin and Maude.*) But although many people in Maine remember Domino's Pizza only for having changed the vessel's name, Domino's should be remembered for having saved the *Victory Chimes*'s life.

In 1990 she came back to Rockland and the windjammer business, and a year later Captains Kip Files and Paul de Gaeta purchased her and rechristened her the *Victory Chimes.* She was designated a National Historic Landmark in 1997 and turned one hundred in 2000, returning to the Chesapeake to celebrate her birthday. During her stay there, then-eighty-seven-year-old William Seaford Stevens came aboard. He had sailed on her during her last years in the cargo business and her first years as a passenger vessel. Captain Files asked what the biggest difference was in her. "She's a darn sight cleaner now," said Captain Stevens.

To this day, she has no inboard auxiliary power; she depends on her yawl boat to move her in close quarters or at times with no wind. As was common on sailing vessels of her day, she does have a 1916 donkey engine forward to power the anchor windlass.

The *Victory Chimes* is no greyhound, but Captain Files says she is a relatively easy boat to sail. Sometimes she seems even longer than she is, though, particularly in tight conditions, and she doesn't stop easily once she's started. She makes a lot of leeway going to weather. But in general she is surprisingly handy. In light airs she'll come about more easily than would a two-master of her size, because the leverage of her mizzen pushes her right through the wind. She likes a good breeze—18 to 20 knots is ideal—and her size and heft make her an impressive lady under way. Captain Files reports that once in a while she can get past even the fastest members of the fleet, if the slant of wind is just right and the breeze is strong enough that they've had to bring in their topsails. "She can make over ten knots—though there's no water left in the bay when we've gone through."

Victory Chimes
Rig: three-masted; bald headed; three headsails
Sail area: 6,500 sq. ft.
Green hull, white waist, red stripe, clipper bow
Length on deck: 132'
Beam: 25'
Draft: 7'6" (18' board down)
Displacement: 395 tons estimated
Power: yawl boat
No. of passengers: 44; crew: 9

Wendameen

The first of many schooner yachts from the drawing board of John Alden, the *Wendameen* was built in East Boothbay, Maine, in 1912. Thought to be one of the earliest yachts to carry auxiliary power, she is heavier and beamier than many of her contemporaries yet still maintains a refined and elegant appearance.

The *Wendameen* was designed for Chester Bliss, owner of the Boston and Albany Railroad and Chapin National Bank. He sailed her on Long Island Sound with his family and friends. In 1916 the *Wendameen* was sold to the Uihlein family of Milwaukee, owners of the Schlitz breweries. With the coming of Prohibition, the *Wendameen* was moved to Chicago, where her new owner was a colorful lawyer named L'Amoreaux, who cruised with his family for ten years. Each year, L'Amoreaux entered the *Wendameen* in the Mackinac race, which took him close to Canada and gave him the opportunity to refill his liquor cabinets. L'Amoreaux brought the *Wendameen* back to Long Island Sound, intending to trade her for a powerboat that better suited his failing health, but he died before the transaction took place. The *Wendameen* became the property of yacht broker G.W. Ford of City Island, New York, who carefully labeled and stored all her gear when he hauled her for the winter at a local yard. The Depression interfered with the resale of the boat. Then came World War II. Ford chose to leave the *Wendameen* laid up rather than allow her to be requisitioned for submarine patrol. He had dreams of retiring onto her and did two major overhauls of the schooner (in 1936 and 1963) at a cost of a quarter of a million

The Wendameen *in the 1920s. Courtesy of Captain Neal Parker.*

dollars. In 1984, when Ford was ninety-two years old, the ship-yard where *Wendameen* had been stored was closed. Ford had neither retired nor ever sailed his schooner, but he abandoned his own hopes and launched her, offering her for sale. The *Wenda-meen* came adrift in a spring storm, suffering serious damage; a purchaser attempted repairs but gave up and left her stuck in a mud bank in western Connecticut.

The *Wendameen's* present owner, Captain Neal Parker, found her in the mud in 1986 as if she were just waiting to make her comeback. He was determined to restore her to her original glory. Although it took years, he accomplished just that. Captain Parker found her gear right where it had been stored by Mr. Ford in 1933. Parker used a great number of the fittings and was even able to utilize one original staysail during his first two sea-sons. Another thread connects her past to her present: a caulker who worked on her in 1936 in City Island. In 1976, while she was still in City Island, his son caulked her; and in 1989 the son, who had since moved to Maine, again worked on her.

Although a great deal of the boat had to be replaced, she exudes much of her early history. The *Wendameen* looks distin-guished with her white hull and varnished cockpit, skylight frames, and trim. Below, as when first launched, the appoint-ments are airy, with white-painted panels and mahogany trim. Simple green velvet cushions in the saloon evoke the charm of an older time.

Captain Parker has collected scrapbooks of pictures and stories about the *Wendameen* and her former owners. He has put them all together in a book and enjoys sharing them as if they were his own memories and not just those of his vessel. "Late at night you feel their shadows around you," he says. An old Victor gramophone is part of the equipment aboard; the George

Gershwin recording of "Rhapsody in Blue" brings applause every time. Captain Parker says the *Wendameen* is a time machine that takes her guests into the early part of the twentieth century for a yachting adventure. Or perhaps it takes them back in their own lives; couples who hadn't thought to hold hands in ten years end up sitting close together alone on deck at night, and social engagements from fifty years back are brought to the minds of more elderly guests.

Sailing is fun on the *Wendameen*. She makes good time in any kind of weather, finding it easy to reach 7 knots and clocking 12 knots on occasion. She likes light air or heavy, though 15 to 20 knots is her choice. As Captain Parker says, today she does "the job she was originally designed for: sailing like a son of a gun and taking people out to have a good time."

Wendameen

Rig: bald headed; round, tapered, extended
    mastheads
Sail area: 2,400 sq. ft.
White hull, bright rail, spoon bow
Length on deck: 67'
Beam: 17'6"
Draft: 9' (full keel)
Displacement: 52 tons
Power: 80-hp diesel
No. of passengers: 14; crew: 4

Identifying the Windjammers

Identifying a vessel can be difficult from a distance, but the more familiar one becomes with large sailing vessels, the easier it is. The sail plan is the clearest identifier; it is the first thing visible, and each vessel's sail plan is just a little different from every other's. Not only is there variety in terms of the particular sails carried—topsails or fishermen staysails, for instance—the balance, lines, proportions, and overall impression are distinctive. Some schooners have very solid-looking rigs, whereas others show more daylight; some have steeper angles to their gaffs, the booms on some extend farther beyond the transom than on others, the relative sizes of mainsail to fore- or headsails are different, and so on.

The following descriptions explain how to distinguish the individual members of the Penobscot Bay windjammer fleet, even from a distance. (See the Glossary, beginning on page 140, for help with terminology.)

Victory Chimes   *Kathryn B.*

A good first step is to count masts. If there are three, and they're all rigged fore and aft, it's *Victory Chimes* or *Kathryn B.* The *Victory Chimes* is far bigger than *Kathryn B.* and has no topmasts. Her fore, main, and mizzen are very nearly the same size, and the gaffs are always perfectly aligned. She has a staysail and inner and outer jibs. *Kathryn B.* has topmasts and sometimes flies topsails. Her mizzen is twice the size of her main and fore. She has a staysail, jib, and flying jib. She is a much smaller vessel than *Victory Chimes.*

If there are square sails, the vessel isn't part of the Penobscot Bay fleet, although several that fly square sails live on the Maine coast or visit regularly.

Angelique

If the vessel has two masts and no yards, the next step is to determine whether it is a schooner or a ketch. Of the Penobscot Bay fleet, only the dark-sailed ketch *Angelique* is not a schooner.

Then, are her main and fore gaff rigged, or does she carry one or more marconi sails or a staysail rig? (Within the fleet, only *Ellida* has a marconi rig.)

Now look for topsails or topmasts. The bald-headed schooners—with no topsails—are *Bowdoin* (the only knockabout in the Penobscot Bay fleet), *American Eagle* (steep spoon

Ellida

bow, very long main boom and correspondingly large mainsail, and extreme sheer), *Wendameen* (spoon bow, mainmast and sail significantly taller than her fore), *J. & E. Riggin* (long, low black hull, spoon bow), *Grace Bailey,* and

Bowdoin

American Eagle

Wendameen

J. & E. Riggin

Grace Bailey

Mercantile

Mercantile. The latter two may be the hardest to differentiate at first, but the proportions of these two clipper-bowed, dark green schooners are different. *Grace Bailey* has a jibboom, *Mercantile* a simple bowsprit. *Grace Bailey* has a noticeably taller rig with raked masts and greater sail area. *Mercantile* has vertical masts and an airier look to her sail plan, with more peak to her gaffs, which are shorter—relative to the respective booms—than are *Grace Bailey*'s.

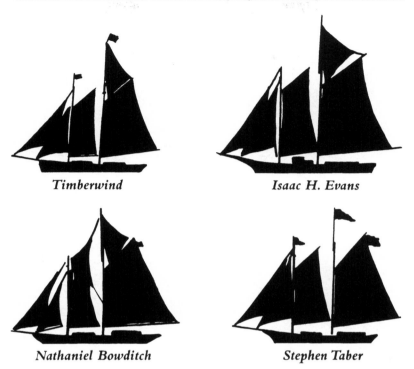

Timberwind   *Isaac H. Evans*

Nathaniel Bowditch   *Stephen Taber*

Carrying a single topmast and topsail are *Timberwind* (spoon bow, leech of topsail nearly a continuation of the line of the main's, and smaller headsails than the others), *Isaac H. Evans* (clipper bow, a more nearly rectangular main, topsail makes a clearly broken line, larger headsails), and *Nathaniel Bowditch* (spoon-bowed black hull, carries a fisherman staysail). The dark green *Stephen Taber* has a single topmast flying a huge pennant but no topsail; her very airy rig has proportionately more boom overhang than any other member of the fleet.

Lewis R. French and *Heritage* have two topmasts and main and jib topsails but no fore topsail. With all sails flying, they look a little as if a tooth were missing. The *French* has a dark gray hull

Lewis R. French   **Heritage**

and a proportionately taller rig, although she's a smaller vessel, whereas *Heritage*'s rig is more stretched out—fore and aft—even relative to her longer hull.

Only *Mary Day* carries main, fore, and jib topsails.

Mary Day

Other Vessels Seen in Maine Waters

Annie McGee, Southwest Harbor, Maine

Pinky, 28' on deck, 9' beam, 6' draft, sail area 800 sq. ft., 11-hp diesel. The *Annie McGee* was built in the 1950s by a Bath Iron Works employee in his spare time. Many of her original fittings were left over from BIW projects, including her ballast—3,500 pounds of cast iron, smuggled out bit by bit in a lunch pail. Launched in 1957, the *Annie McGee* never made the trip to Europe that her builder intended, though he sailed her for nearly twenty years before he died. In 1986 her present owner, Captain "Yo" Yosarian, bought her. She is one of the few vessels on the Maine coast to sport an oculus, an eye painted on her bow, which is a traditional sign of good luck in the Far East. The *Annie McGee* carries six passengers and is available for day charters.

Appledore, Portsmouth, New Hampshire

Staysail schooner, 49' on deck, 12'6" beam, 6'6" draft, 16 tons gross, sail area 1,400 sq. ft. (in marconi main, staysail, two head-sails, and fisherman), 25-hp diesel. The first of Herb Smith's six schooners (five named *Appledore*), she was designed by D. C. "Bud" McIntosh and built of native New Hampshire woods by him and Smith. She was launched in 1972 and taken to the West Indies for the making of the video *Romantic Caribbean Islands.* Captain Smith sold her in 1977; presently she is owned by Captain Rick Bates and is available for a variety of trips.

Appledore [II], Camden, Maine

Schooner, 65' on deck, 19' beam, 9'6" draft, 67 tons displace-ment, sail area 2,070 sq. ft. in the four lowers (carries topsail sometimes), Cummins diesel. The hull of Captain Herb Smith's second schooner designed by Bud McIntosh was built in 1978 at the Harvey Gamage yard in South Bristol, Maine. She was fit-ted out by Captain Smith, who made a global circumnavigation with her before she was put into day and charter work.

Accommodates 26 overnight and 49 on day sails, which she now offers out of Camden in summer and, sometimes, Key West in winter.

Bay Lady, Bar Harbor, Maine

Steel schooner, 65' on deck, 18' beam, 6'6" draft. Built in 1988 in East Boothbay, Maine, specifically for the short-trip passenger business. Owned by Frenchman Bay Company.

*Courtesy of the Nova Scotia Depart-
ment of Tourism and Culture.*

Bluenose II, Halifax, Nova Scotia

143' on deck, 27' beam, 16' draft, 285 tons displacement, sail area 12,550 sq. ft. (in main, foresail, three headsails, two topsails, and fisherman), two Caterpillar diesels. Built in 1960 in Lunenburg, Nova Scotia, as a private yacht for Olands Ltd. Beer Brewers, she is a reproduction in hull and rig of the original *Bluenose,* generally accepted to have been the fastest of the racing fishermen. These racing vessels were better sailers but poorer freighters than the typical fuller-formed fishing schooners. *Bluenose II* has been clocked at 18 knots under sail; her engines allow her to cruise at 12 knots. She is constructed of native softwoods with the exception of her keel and stem, which are of good oak left over from the construction at the same yard of the reproduction *Bounty* for the movie *Mutiny on the Bounty.* This hardwood backbone has made possible a longer life than might otherwise have been the case, because native softwoods are not long-lasting. *Bluenose II* was donated to the province of Nova Scotia in 1971 and is used to promote the province for business and tourism.

Photo by Neil Irons.

Bonnie Lynn, Islesboro, Maine

Steel brigantine, 57' on deck, 15'3" beam, 6'6" draft, sail area 2,075 sq. ft., 220-hp diesel. Formerly a topsail schooner, but re-rigged in 2001 as a brigantine, the elegantly appointed *Bonnie Lynn* is available for charter and works from Islesboro in summer and the Caribbean in winter under her owners Captains Earl and Bonnie MacKenzie. She is certified for 38 passengers coastal and 10 for ocean sailing, though the MacKenzies prefer to have no more than 7 guests.

Bounty, Greenport, New York

Full-rigged ship, 120' on deck, 30' beam, 13' draft, 550 tons displacement, sail area 10,000 sq. ft. (in eighteen or more sails), twin diesels. Built at the Smith and Ruhland yard in Lunenburg, Nova Scotia, to sail to Tahiti, where she was a prop for the 1962 movie *Mutiny on the Bounty,* starring Marlon Brando, and also acted as

Courtesy of MediaConcepts.

supply vessel and electricity generator for the film company. She was to be burned in the course of making the movie, but the story is that Brando refused to finish work on the film if she were destroyed. MGM kept her as a shoreside attraction in St. Petersburg for twenty years; then Ted Turner found he had purchased her along with MGM's film library in 1985. She was in two more movies before being donated to a nonprofit group in Fall River, Massachusetts. At this writing she is in Maine having serious work done for a new owner; it is planned that she will go to work from Greenport, Long Island, and will be moving around the coast from time to time.

Brilliant, Mystic, Connecticut

Marconi-main schooner, 61'6" on deck, 14'8" beam, 8'10" draft, 37 tons displacement, sail area 2,417 sq. ft. (in four lowers and fisherman), diesel auxiliary. *Brilliant* was designed by Sparkman & Stephens and built at the Nevins yard on City Island, New York, in 1932. Although designed for deepwater cruising, she was a competitive racer as well. In 1933 she made a trans-

Atlantic passage in record time for a vessel her size, averaging more than 9 knots the whole way. Originally gaff rigged on main and fore, she was re-rigged with her present marconi main after World War II, during which period she served on submarine patrol. She is now operated by Mystic Seaport as a sail training vessel.

Corwith Cramer, Woods Hole, Massachusetts

Steel brigantine, 98' on deck, 26' beam, 13' draft, 280 tons displacement, sail area 7,800 sq. ft., 500-hp diesel. She was built in

1987 in Spain for the Sea Education Association, the present owners, and logs an average of 10,000 nautical miles each year. She carries 36, including 10 professional staff (captain, mates, engineer, steward, and scientists). She holds enough stores for six weeks at sea. Including fuel, water, food, and the people themselves, she puts on some 60 tons before departure. The Sea Education Association offers college-level, semester-long oceanography and maritime programs as well as shorter educational seminars for a variety of participants.

Courtesy of Captain Herb Smith.

Eastwind, Boothbay Harbor, Maine

Marconi-main schooner, 56' on deck, 14' beam, 6'6" draft, 25 tons displacement, sail area 1,600 sq. ft. Captain Herb and Doris Smith's sixth schooner, she was built by them in their backyard over the course of three years and launched in 1999; she is a sister to their *Appledore III,* designed by Bud McIntosh. The Smiths have sailed her to South America and back and now are offering day sails from Boothbay Harbor.

Ernestina, New Bedford, Massachusetts

106' on deck, 24'5" beam, 13' draft, 240 tons displacement, sail area 8,323 sq. ft. (including flying jib, main and fore topsails, and fisherman). Formerly the *Effie C. Morrissey,* she was designed by George M. McClain and built in Essex, Massachusetts, in 1894; she is the oldest surviving Grand Banks fishing schooner. Although supposedly built along the lines of the Gloucester fishing schooner *Fredonia,* in fact she's more of a workhorse. She fished the Grand Banks for eighteen years, bringing in up to 200,000 pounds of fish each trip. She was later converted to carry cargo on the Labrador run. In 1924 she was purchased by Robert A. Bartlett, who made twenty exploratory voyages to the Arctic with her; in 1940 she reached 80° 22' north latitude, the farthest north of any wooden sailing vessel. After service off Greenland in World War II and a brief and disastrous career as a private yacht, in 1948 she was taken to the Cape Verde Islands, where she was renamed *Ernestina* and used as a general carrier into the mid-1960s. Among other payloads were the last immigrants—and perhaps the only voluntary black immigrants—to arrive in the United States in a commercial sailing vessel. After suffering serious damage in 1976, she was rebuilt by the Cape Verdians with the help of some of the Americans who as young men had sailed aboard her in the Arctic. She was donated to the United States by the new West African Republic of Cape Verde in 1982. The Commonwealth of Massachusetts now owns the vessel and runs a variety of educational programs with additional private funding.

Gazela Philadelphia, Philadelphia, Pennsylvania

Barkentine, 140' on deck, 177' overall, 27' beam, 17' draft, 652 tons displacement, sail area 11,000 sq. ft. (in sixteen sails), 385-hp auxiliary diesel engine. The last of the wooden Portuguese sailing fishermen, she is the largest original wooden square-rigger still sailing. Her records date back only to 1901, when she was built in her present configuration; her history prior to that time isn't entirely known. There is some evidence she may have been built in 1883, or perhaps she was constructed of timbers from a vessel built in that year. In any case, *Gazela* sailed from Portugal to the Grand Banks for six months every year from

1901 through 1969, carrying forty men and thirty-five dories and bringing back as much as 350 tons of salt fish each trip. In 1971 she was purchased to become Philadelphia's Tall Ship. She had significant rebuilding in 1992 and her deck was rebuilt in 2001, but she has always been copper clad below the waterline, and her planking is still in excellent condition. She was constructed of "stone pine" and "maritime pine," which some believe had been planted by Portugal's Prince Henry the Navigator in the fifteenth century. Today she sails with a crew of 24 to 36, all of them volunteers except for the captain and mate. She is owned and operated by the nonprofit Philadelphia Ship Preservation Guild.

Harvey Gamage, Islesboro, Maine

Schooner, 95' on deck, 24' beam, 10' draft, sail area 4,200 sq. ft., 220-hp diesel. She was built in 1973 for the passenger trade at the Harvey Gamage yard in South Bristol, Maine, using the same lofting as the *Bill of Rights*. She is now operated by the nonprofit Ocean Classroom Foundation, which offers "structured sea adventure expeditions with academic studies." She sails with up to 27 students and 9 crew/faculty.

Courtesy of Tall Ship NewsWire.

Highlander Sea, Halifax, Nova Scotia

Schooner, approximately 116' on deck, 25'2" beam, 14' draft, 241 tons displacement, sail area 10,000 sq. ft. (in 4 lowers and 3 topsails), two diesels. Designed by Starling Burgess to race for the Fisherman's Cup competition between Canadian and Gloucester fishing schooners, she was built at the James and Tarr yard in Essex, Massachusetts, but the races were canceled prior to her completion. The Boston pilots had her finished, giving her the name *Pilot,* and she served the port of Boston for more than fifty years. She now belongs to Secunda Marine of Nova Scotia, which uses her for sail training and marine awareness programs.

Kalmar Nyckel, Wilmington, Delaware

93' overall and on deck, 25' beam, 12' draft, 298 tons displacement, sail area 7,600 sq. ft., two 180-hp diesels. She is a re-creation of the seventeenth-century Dutch pinnace that brought the first European settlers from Sweden to the Delaware Valley, making

Photo by Chris Queeney.

four trips starting in 1637. The goal of the Kalmar Nyckel Foundation, which owns the modern vessel, is to promote awareness of the colonial roots and maritime history of Wilmington.

Larinda, Cape Cod, Massachusetts

Ferro-cement junk-rigged schooner, 56' on deck, 16'6" beam, 8' draft, sail area 2,800 sq. ft., auxiliary engine (7-ton restored 1928 Wolverine diesel, 2,200 cu. in., providing 100 hp). Her keel was laid in 1970 in owner/captain Larry Mahan's backyard in Marston Mills, Massachusetts, and she was launched in 1996. More than a thousand volunteers were involved in her building, many leaving special touches behind, including a magnificent array of wood carvings inside and out. The schooner was designed along the lines of an eighteenth-century schooner but

was junk rigged for ease of construction, light weight, and ease of handling. She is available for charter, special events, and educational programs with organized groups, and participates in many historic reenactments and Tall Ship gatherings.

Lazy Jack, Camden, Maine

Schooner, 36'8" on deck, 11' beam, 6' draft, documented at 9 tons. Fashioned after the *Fredonia*-style schooners, she was built in 1947 in Ipswich, Massachusetts, by Fred Whittier, who had been a shipbuilder at the famed A. D. Story yard in Essex. She

spent the 1950s in the Bahamas on charters and day sails. Before coming to Camden, she was in Kennebunkport, where in 1988 she was 90 percent rebuilt at the Landing School. Captain Sean O'Connor has been offering day sails aboard *Lazy Jack* from Camden since 1998.

Lettie G. Howard, New York, New York

Schooner, 86' on deck, 21'1" beam, 10'6" draft, 102 tons displacement, sail area 5,017 sq. ft. (with main topsail and fisherman), twin 85-hp diesels. The *Howard* was built in 1893 at the A. D. Story yard in Essex, Massachusetts, on the *Fredonia* model. She fished from Gloucester for eight years, then moved to Pensacola, Florida; under the name *Mystic C,* she fished for red snapper for fifty-five years off Mexico. She was given an auxiliary engine in 1923. South Street Seaport Museum in New York City bought her in 1966; she was named a National Historic Landmark in 1988 and underwent full restoration in the early 1990s. She can carry 13 students and 7 crew. Although she is still owned by South Street, in recent years she has been chartered by the Ocean Classroom Foundation.

Lynx, Portsmouth, New Hampshire

76' on deck, 23' beam, 8'6" draft, 98.6 tons displacement, sail area 4,669 sq. ft. Launched in 2001 at Rockport Marine in Rockport, Maine, the Melbourne Smith–designed *Lynx* represents a privateer from the War of 1812 and operates as much as is feasible in the style of those times, with her crew dressed in period uniforms. She is owned by Woods Maritime, whose executive director, Woodson Woods, says she is "dedicated to the instruction of students in the honorable tradition of the sea."

Maine, Bath, Maine

Pinky, 39' on deck, 13' beam, 6' draft, sail area approximately 1,000 sq. ft., diesel auxiliary. Launched in 1985, she is owned by

and was built at the Maine Maritime Museum in Bath from a half model of a pinky built in East Boothbay in the 1830s; she is typical of the type as to rig, deck, and details. She is on display and occasionally sailed by volunteers and staff in festivities up and down the Maine coast.

Courtesy of Captain Steve Pagels.

Malabar, Cherryfield, Maine

Ferro-cement schooner, 65' on deck, 21' beam, 8' draft, approximately 100 tons displacement, sail area 3,000 sq. ft. Built as the *Rachel & Ebenezer* at Long Beach Shipyard, Bath, Maine, in 1975, she is now owned by Captain Steve Pagels's Downeast Windjammer Cruises. She is usually operated out of Greenport, Long Island, but appears in Maine from time to time.

Margaret Todd, Cherryfield, Maine

Four-masted steel schooner, 121' on deck, 23' beam, 5'9" draft (12' boards down), 150 tons displacement, sail area 4,800 sq. ft. in nine sails. Named for owner Captain Steve Pagels's grand-

Courtesy of Captain Steve Pagels.

mother, the *Margaret Todd* was built in St. Augustine, Florida, for the day-sailing trade. She was launched in 1998 and sails from Bar Harbor.

Mistress, Camden, Maine

Schooner, 46' on deck, 13'6" beam, 6' draft, sail area 1,170 sq. ft. (in four sails), diesel auxiliary. Her construction was begun in 1960 on Deer Isle as a backyard project by a man who planned to use her privately. She was purchased by Maine Windjammer Cruises in 1966 and fitted out for three couples in separate cabins, each with its own head. Over the years the *Mistress* has been

owned by the various owners of the "green boats" (presently Captain Ray Williamson). The *Mistress* is often the first command for newly licensed captains, including, in 2001, Captain Williamson's daughter Allysa. The little schooner was lengthened 6 feet in 1992 as part of a full rebuild.

Niagara, Erie, Pennsylvania

Brig, 116' on deck, 32' beam, 10' draft, 297 tons displacement, sail area 12,665 sq. ft., twin diesels. Originally built in Erie during the War of 1812, the *Niagara* was Commander Oliver Hazard Perry's relief flagship in the Battle of Lake Erie in 1813. Aboard her, he broke the British battle line, forcing the surrender of the British naval forces. It was from the deck of the *Niagara* that Perry sent the famous message, "We have met the enemy, and they are ours." She served but seven years longer, then was scuttled. In commemoration of the battle, she was raised and fully rebuilt in the early 1900s. After reconstruction in 1988 to plans by naval architect Melbourne Smith, a few original timbers and parts still remained. She serves today as the flagship of the state of Pennsylvania. Although the original vessel carried 155 men in 1813, today she sails with a professional crew of 12 to 16, and 20 volunteers.

Norfolk Rebel, Norfolk, Virginia

Schooner-rigged "tugantine," 59' on deck, sail area 1,300 sq. ft. (with traditional gaff main and foresails, square sail, modern genoa headsail, and spinnaker), 320 hp. She can make a whopping 5.5 knots under full sail if she has breeze enough. Her bowsprit retracts back inside the hull so she can push. Built in 1980 in response to the energy crisis, the working tug was designed from the start as a sail-assist vessel. She works out of Norfolk doing coastal towing and salvage; she has also fished, long-lining, along the East Coast and Gulf of Mexico. After the 1999 season, she towed *Victory Chimes* home to the Chesapeake, where the *Chimes* celebrated her hundredth birthday. *Norfolk Rebel's* captain, Lane Briggs, visits Penobscot Bay regularly and joins in organized events for schooners and other large sailing vessels.

Olad, Camden, Maine

Schooner, 47' on deck, 12'6" beam, 6'6" draft, sail area 1,500 sq. ft., diesel auxiliary. The *Olad* was designed by Chester A. Crosby

as the private yacht *Whistle Binkie* and was launched from his family's yard in Osterville, Massachusetts, in 1928. Later she was in the charter trade in the Caribbean and Bermuda. Since 1987, under the ownership of the Nugent family, she has been giving day sails from Camden for up to 21 passengers at a time.

Picton Castle, Lunenburg, Nova Scotia

Riveted-steel three-masted barque, 135' on deck, 24' beam, 14'6" draft, sail area 14,450 sq. ft., 690-hp Burmeister & Wain

Courtesy of Tall Ship NewsWire.

Alpha diesel. Built in 1928 as a fishing trawler, the *Picton Castle* operated out of Wales, served the Royal Navy as a minesweeper in World War II, and totally by happenstance was named "the liberator of Norway." She hauled freight in the North and Baltic Seas. In 1996 her present owner, Daniel Morland, brought her to Lunenburg for a total refit into the barque she is today. He made one circumnavigation of the globe and was partway along in a second at this writing. The *Picton Castle* carries 17 professional crew and 23 paying amateurs.

Pride of Baltimore II, Baltimore, Maryland

Topsail schooner, 96'6" on deck and 173' overall, 26' beam, 12'4" draft, 185.5 tons displacement, sail area 10,000 sq. ft. (in eleven sails), twin Caterpillar diesels. Designed by Thomas C. Gillmer after the Baltimore clippers of the early nineteenth century, and built to replace the original *Pride of Baltimore,* lost at sea in 1986, the *Pride of Baltimore II* conforms to Coast Guard regulations for carrying passengers. With a professional paid crew of 12, the *Pride* has toured all over the world as a goodwill ambassador for the city of Baltimore and the state of Maryland, promoting economic development and tourism. The extreme rake of the masts of the Baltimore clippers is distinctive.

Providence, Providence, Rhode Island

Topsail sloop, 60' on deck and 110' overall, 20' beam, 10' draft, sail area 3,470 sq. ft. (in main, topsail, staysail, three headsails, and main course). The original *Providence* was built at a time when the British wouldn't allow the American colonists to build a vessel more than 60 feet long. Built as the merchant vessel *Katy,* she was 60 feet long but just as deep and broad as a vessel that size could reasonably be, and she carried a rig that made her 110 feet overall. She was known to be lucky, winning more than forty Revolutionary War battles. Today's *Providence* replica was built in 1976 in Rhode Island. She has a fiberglass hull but certainly maintains an old-vessel character. Much of her wood is old; her decking, for instance, was part of a 200-year-old warehouse. Her owner, the Providence Maritime Heritage Foundation, offers a number of educational and corporate programs.

Rachel B. Jackson, Rockland, Maine

Topsail schooner, 55' on deck, 16' beam, 8' draft, 52 tons gross, sail area 2,500 sq. ft. (including main and jib topsails, square sail, and fisherman), 115-hp Westerbeke diesel. The *Rachel B. Jackson* was constructed in the traditional manner from plans drafted in

1890. Her hull was built in Jonesport, Maine. She was finished by George Emery, who was then in Freeport, and launched in 1982. She was operated as a sail training vessel by Mystic Seaport in Mystic, Connecticut, then sold to an individual who made a three-year circumnavigation of the world in her. Since 1992 she has been carrying passengers, most recently from Rockland in summer and the Caribbean in winter. She is owned by Andrew and Steven Keblinsky.

Roald Amundsen, Woljast, Germany

Steel brig, 139' on deck, 25' beam, 15' draft, 252 tons gross, sail area 9,265 sq. ft., 300-hp diesel. She was built in 1952 as a motor-

tanker for the East German navy. After reunification, she was bought by the nonprofit LebenlernenaufSegelschiffen (Learning to Live on Sailing Ships) and converted to the traditional square rig that she carries now. This rig requires full participation of all aboard, making a complete sailing experience and giving true responsibility to students. Complying with the German high safety standards for traditional sail training vessels, the *Amundsen* is licensed for worldwide voyaging. In Maine she has been working with Hurricane Island Outward Bound School in Rockland. She carries a crew of 14 and can accommodate 32 trainees overnight.

Robert C. Seamans, Woods Hole, Massachusetts
Steel brigantine, 114'4" on deck, 25'4" beam, 12'3" draft, 300 tons displacement, sail area 8,554 sq. ft. Designed by Laurent Giles and

Courtesy of the Sea Education Association.

built in Tacoma, Washington, the *Seamans* was launched in 2001. She belongs to the Sea Education Association (see *Corwith Cramer*) and carries a staff of 10 (sailing and educators) and 25 students.

Sherman Zwicker, Boothbay Harbor, Maine

Grand Banks schooner, 142' on deck, 26' beam, 13'6" draft, huge 320-hp Fairbanks Morse engine. One of the last Grand Banks schooners built (in the same yard as the *Bluenose*), the *Zwicker* is typical of the Canadian fish freighters, being fuller forward and in the forefoot than the racing *Bluenose*. She was launched in Lunenburg, Nova Scotia, in 1942. Although she carried steadying sails for her short knockabout rig, her main source of power was her engine, which to this day drives the propeller directly, with no gearbox. (To go backward, the crew must shut down the engine, reverse the cam, and restart.) The *Zwicker* fished until the late 1960s, carrying 24 fisherman, 12 dories, and a crew of 4 (captain, engineer, cook, and boy.) Her hold had a capacity of 320,000 pounds of fish, and she carried even more stacked on deck. She made three trips to the Grand Banks each year, and in fall and winter carried salt fish to South America, bringing salt back to preserve the next season's catch.

The *Sherman Zwicker* is now maintained for display by the Grand Banks Schooner Museum of Boothbay. When she isn't at various festivities on the East Coast and in the Maritimes, she is often berthed at the Maine Maritime Museum in Bath.

Spirit of Massachusetts, Boston, Massachusetts

Schooner, 100' on deck, 24' beam, 10'6" draft, 138 tons displacement, sail area 7,000 sq. ft. (with main, fore, and jib topsails and fisherman), 250-hp diesel. Launched at Charlestown Navy Yard in 1984, she is modeled on the lines of the *Fredonia,* the famous Gloucester fisherman schooner of 1889. Always sailed with an educational mission, she is now owned and operated by the Ocean Classroom Foundation. (See *Harvey Gamage,* page 117.) She carries 22 students and 9 crew/faculty.

Summertime, Brooklin, Maine

Pinky, 52'9" on deck, 13'7" beam, 7' draft, 37 tons displacement, sail area 1,700 sq. ft. (in three lower sails; sometimes flies a fisher-

man), diesel auxiliary engine. She was built in the traditional manner from lines that Howard Chapelle took off a model in Portland dating to the 1830s. *Summertime* is ruggedly constructed of the same types of wood as early-nineteenth-century pinkies: native oak, tamarack, and locust. She is the largest pinky sailing today and probably one of the larger ones ever built. Captains Bill Brown and George Allen and a number of young volunteers constructed her over the course of several winters, launching her in 1986. Licensed for 7 passengers overnight, 20 day-sailing. Captain Brown sails her on a variety of trips from several harbors each summer.

Surprise, Camden, Maine

Schooner, 44' on deck, 12' beam, 6'7" draft, sail area 970 sq. ft., diesel auxiliary. The *Surprise* was designed by Thomas McManus, innovative designer of fishing schooners, and built in 1918 in Rockport, Massachusetts, as a private yacht for Martin Kattenhorn, who sailed and raced her from Long Island Sound for forty-five years. She has never been known by another name, but she has lived in Penobscot Bay before, as a member of the Porter family of Great Spruce Head Island. Current owners Cap-

tain Jack and Barbara Moore live aboard her in summer and have been offering day sails on her from Camden since 1986.

Sylvina Beal, Cherryfield, Maine

Knockabout schooner, 80' on deck, 17'3" beam, 8' draft, 60 tons displacement, sail area 2,200 sq. ft. (in a bald-headed rig), 80-hp Perkins diesel. Oak on oak, treenail fastened, she was built in 1911 in East Boothbay, Maine, as an auxiliary schooner sardine carrier. In the mid-1930s, her sail area was cut back and she was

Courtesy of Captain Steve Pagels.

given a larger engine and a wheelhouse. For more than sixty years she worked in various aspects of the fishing business, carrying fish and other products out of ports from Nova Scotia to Massachusetts. In the late 1970s, she was entirely rebuilt to carry sardines to a Canadian-owned packing plant planned for Rockland. When the plant didn't open, the *Beal* was seized for unpaid debt. Captain John Worth bought her in 1980, restored her sailing rig, replaced her huge diesel engines with a small auxiliary, and installed passenger accommodations. She has worked in the passenger trade out of Belfast and Mystic and now, as a member of Steve Pagels's fleet, Boothbay Harbor.

Tabor Boy, Marion, Massachusetts

Steel schooner, 92' on deck, 21'9" beam, 10'6" draft, 160 tons displacement, sail area 3,500 sq. ft., 330-hp diesel. Built in Amsterdam in 1914, she worked as a Dutch North Sea pilot schooner until 1929; she carries a "2" on her mainsail in honor of that assignment. Under the name of *Bestevaer,* she sailed as a Dutch Merchant Service school ship and in World War II was captured by the Germans during their occupation of the Netherlands. Returned to Holland after the war, she was purchased by

American Ralph C. Allen, who presented her to Tabor Academy of Marion, Massachusetts, in 1954. The academy has sailed her since then in a variety of programs in Marion, the Caribbean, and Maine. She has berths for 22, including 6 crew, who, except for foreign trips, are older Tabor Academy students.

Westward, Woods Hole, Massachusetts

Steel staysail schooner, 95' on deck, 21'6" beam, 12'6" draft, 250 tons displacement, sail area 7,000 sq. ft. (including a single square topsail), 500-hp diesel. The *Westward* was designed along the lines of a North Sea pilot schooner by Eldridge-McInnis and built as a yacht in 1961. She has been owned and operated since 1972 by the Sea Education Association (see *Corwith Cramer,* page 113). She carries 35, including 10 professional staff.

When and If, Vineyard Haven, Massachusetts

Marconi-main schooner, 63'5" on deck, 15'1" beam, 8'6" draft, sail area 1,771 sq. ft., General Motors 4-71 diesel auxiliary. Designed by John Alden, she was built in Wiscasset, Maine, for then-Colonel George S. Patton and launched in 1939. Carrying a

square sail and flying jib as originally rigged, she now has a marconi main, gaff fore, two headsails, and a fisherman. Although she never carried General Patton around the world, as planned, she remained in his family until the 1970s, when she was donated to the Landmark School, which used her in its program for dyslexic students. (Patton had been dyslexic himself.) She was so seriously damaged in a storm in 1990 that she was feared beyond repair, but her original construction was sufficiently strong that rebuilding was possible and justified. A three-year rebuild was completed by Gannon and Benjamin of Vineyard Haven, who now own her with Jim Mairs and Gina Webster of New York City. They manage her today for charter, which often includes educational programs.

Updates on vessels that have worked in Maine waters recently or appeared in earlier editions of *Windjammer Watching:*

Adventure, 121' knockabout schooner, 1926. The last dory-fishing schooner out of Gloucester, she is dockside in Gloucester, Massachusetts; her owners' goal is to restore her and return her to active sailing as a floating classroom as well as a lasting tribute to the fishing heritage of Gloucester and Essex County.

Appledore V, 58' steel schooner, 1992. Now called *Westwind* and belonging to Traverse Tall Ship Company, she is giving day sails on Lake Michigan from Traverse City.

Bill of Rights, 95' schooner, 1971. Built as a yacht by Harvey Gamage in South Bristol, Maine, she has moved to the Los Angeles Maritime Institute in San Pedro, California.

Flying Fish, 45' schooner, 1936. Now returned to her original purpose as a private yacht, hailing from Camden, Maine.

Francis Todd, 78' schooner, 1947. Now called *Aurora* and operating out of Newport, Rhode Island.

"HMS" Rose, 135' full-rigged ship, 1970. Launched in Lunenburg, Nova Scotia, in 1970 and rebuilt in Bridgeport, Connecticut, in the 1980s. She was purchased by Seven Seas Ventures, Inc., of Newport, Rhode Island, and at this writing was scheduled to appear in a movie based on one or more Patrick O'Brian novels.

Natalie Todd, 101' three-masted schooner, 1941. Now known as *American Pride,* she is owned by the American Heritage Marine Institute in Long Beach, California. She is available for charter and educational programs.

New Way, 92' schooner, 1939. Once again known as *Western Union,* she has returned to Key West, where she is available for private charter and day trips.

North Wind, 57' steel schooner, 1995. Sold to Philadelphia City Sail. She is involved with educational programs there.

Ocean Star, 74' steel schooner, 1991. She now belongs to Argo Academy of Sarasota, Florida. She sails in the Caribbean, serving as a classroom for an alternative high school program.

Roseway, 112' schooner, 1925. For sale as of this writing.

Glossary of Nautical Terms

Aft: toward the rear of the boat; astern

Athwartships: across the vessel

Bald headed: having no topsails

Barkentine: vessel of three or more masts, the foremost of which carries square sails; the others are fore-and-aft rigged

Beam: breadth of the vessel

Bilge: lowest part of the vessel's interior

Billet head: wooden scroll used in place of a figurehead

Block: pulley used in a vessel's rig

Boomkin: support for rigging extending beyond the transom

Bow: forward part of a vessel

Bowsprit: spar extending forward of the hull onto which headsails are attached

Brig: two-masted vessel, square sails on each mast

Brigantine: two-masted vessel, the foremost carrying square sails, the main fore-and-aft rigged

Bright: finished with varnish as opposed to paint

Bulkhead: vertical partition that strengthens or divides the hull

Bulwark: inside of a vessel's hull above the deck

Ceiling: planking on the inside of the frame

Centerboard: board that can be lowered to provide resistance to the sideways movement of a vessel, as does a keel, but with the advantage that it can be raised to allow the vessel to navigate shallow water

Centerboard trunk: box into which the centerboard is raised

Chain plate: fitting on the side of a vessel to which the shrouds are secured

Club: spar on the foot of a jib or headsail

Coach house: small structure on deck over the companionway

Coaster: vessel that carried cargo from one coastal port to another; not a deepwater vessel

Companionway: ladder or stairway from deck to quarters below

Crosstrees: horizontal pieces on the mast to spread the shrouds (rigging)

Davits: arms extending over the side or stern to carry a small boat

Displacement: actual weight of a vessel (measured in long tons by the weight of water she displaces when floating)

Donkey engine: engine on deck that provides power for raising the anchor or sails or lifting cargo; does not provide power to propel the vessel

Draft: vertical distance from the surface of the water to the deepest part of the vessel's keel

Eastern-rig dragger: fishing vessel that sets dragging gear off the side of the vessel (as opposed to western draggers, which are stern rigged)

Fathom: 6 feet

Feathering props: propellers with blades that rotate on their individual axes when not in use in order to decrease water resistance

Fisherman: quadrilateral staysail between the foremast and the mainmast above a gaff-rigged fore sail

Fly rail: open rail around the quarterdeck

Flying jib: jib topsail

Fo'c'sle (forecastle): cabin farthest forward, often the crew's quarters

Fore: toward the bow of the vessel

Fore-and-aft sails: sails set from a vertical mast or stay, the normal position being parallel to the keel, as opposed to square rigged

Forefoot: forward section of a full keel

Freeboard: portion of the hull above water

Gaff rig: quadrilateral lower sails, luff attached to a mast, with a spar above (gaff) and usually a boom below

Galley: kitchen

Gam: vessels tied together for a visit or friendly get-together

Genoa: broad jib whose leech is vertical or angled beyond vertical, overlapping the sail or sails aft of it

Going to weather: see "on the wind"

Halyard: line used to hoist sails, flags, or spars

Head: toilet

Headsails: all triangular sails set ahead of the foremast

Heel: to lean at an angle when sailing

Hog: sagging of the bow and stern of an aging vessel. In an extreme case, the profile appears to arch like a hog's back. Used as a verb or noun.

Holding ground: ocean bottom in which a vessel is anchored

Jibboom: spar extending beyond the bowsprit

Junk rig: sail rig of Chinese origin, featuring sails with a number of horizontal battens crossing the mast

Kedge: to move a vessel by laying out an anchor and hauling the vessel toward it

Keel: main structural member down the centerline of a vessel's hull, or the lowest part of a hull

Ketch: two-masted vessel whose after mast is shorter than the forward one (main) and ahead of the rudder post

Knockaboat: vessel whose jib stay attaches at the bow with no bowsprit

Knot: measure of speed; one knot is equal to 6,080.2 feet (one nautical mile, or one minute of latitude) per hour

Leech: after edge of a sail rigged fore and aft, or outer edge of a square sail

Leeward: away from the wind

Leeway: motion of a vesel to leeward, caused by the wind

Lowers: lower sails of a vessel that might carry topsails

Luff: (n) forward part of a sail; (v) to shake, as with an improperly trimmed sail

Main course: bottom square sail on the main mast

Marconi: triangular sail, luff attached to a mast (as opposed to gaff rigged)

Mayday: emergency call

Off the wind: sailing downwind

On the wind: sailing on as close a course as possible to the direction from which the wind is coming

Peak: highest point of gaff-rigged sail, at after end of gaff

Pinky: early, small shore-fishing schooner, distinctive for its characteristic high and narrow stern

Port: left-hand side of a vessel, looking forward

Rake: degree to which a mast tilts from perpendicular

Reach: to sail across the wind

Reef: to lessen the area of a sail, usually by tying down a portion of it

Scantlings: dimensions of a vessel's framing

Schooner: vessel with two or more masts, with the after mast as tall as or taller than the other(s)

Sheer, sheerline: curve in the profile of the upper edge of a boat's hull

Shoal draft: vessel that requires little depth of water to float

Shorten sail: to reef or take down sails or replace them with smaller ones

Six-pack: slang term for a boat that, because it carries no more than six passengers, requires no Coast Guard inspection

Snatch block: block that opens so a line may be fed through it easily

Square rigged: sails rigged across the vessel on yards centered on a mast

Starboard: right-hand side of a vessel, looking forward

Staysail rig: schooner with (usually) triangular sails hung from a stay in place of a gaff or marconi foresail. See *Appledore* [I].

Stem: foremost upright timber of a wooden boat

Stern: after or rear section of the boat

Stiff: takes a breeze without heeling to any great degree

Strake: plank or planks running the length of a vessel's hull

Transom: athwartships, flattened part of the stern

Treenail fastened: timbers and planks joined by wedged wooden pegs (rather than metal fastenings)

Trim: to adjust the sails according to wind direction

Whitehall: long, narrow, graceful rowing boat

Windlass: device for bringing in the anchor chain

Windward: weather side, or side toward the wind

Wing and wing, "wung out": with the wind coming from dead astern, sailing with at least one sail set on each side of the vessel, spread like wings

Yard: horizontal spar from which a square sail is hung

Yawl boat: small powerboat that provides propulsion for a sailing vessel

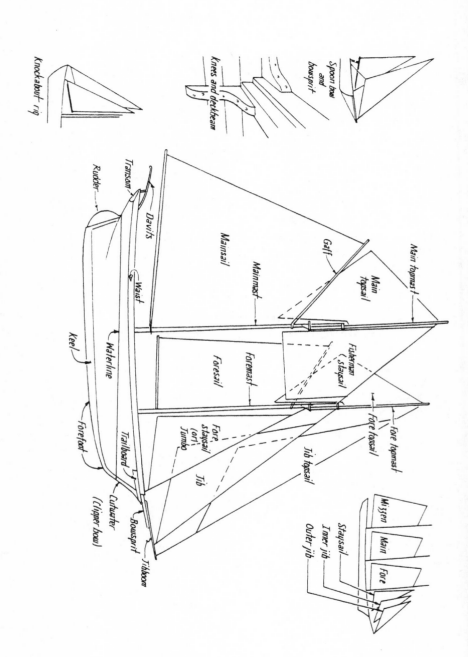

Knockabout rig

Spoon bow and bowsprit

Knees and deckbeam

Rudder

Transom

Davits

Mainsail

Mainmast

Gaff

Main topsail

Main topmast

Waist

Foresail

Foremast

Fisherman staysail

Fore topmast

Fore topsail

Keel

Waterline

Jib topsail

Forefoot

Trailboard

Fore staysail (or) Jumbo

Jib

Cutwater (Clipper bow)

Bowsprit

Jibboom

Mizzen

Main

Fore

Staysail

Inner jib

Outer jib

45279669R00087

Made in the USA
Middletown, DE
01 July 2017